A Freestyle Life

Clint Ewing

Thank you for the support! — Clint Ewing

THANK YOU

Special thanks to those who have believed in me from the start and made it possible for me to do what I do. Bruce Parker, Phillip Mayfield, Ben Ewing, Sampas Family, Kendra Bess Moore, Laura Morgan, Dunlop tires, Barbie Howard, Tucker Rocky, Chris Guadagnini, Rie Desko, Kelli Hagen, Matt Quinn, Brad Brenner, Gannon Boyd, Jeff Restivo, Mike Shapiro and for the gift of life Kris & Irene Ewing

Dedicated to Norris Ewing

CONTENTS

1 FAST LIFE

My life moves fast: fast cars, fast bikes, and faster women. I am hurtling through the sky halfway across the Pacific Ocean on a plane to Guam, but here in the cabin, time is standing still. And today that's ok, I am surrounded by seven beautiful women for thirteen hours, life is good.

How did I get to the point in my life to be hired and flown across the Pacific to perform stunts on a motorcycle?

It started at the age of eight, when I acquired my first motorcycle. I enjoyed playing sports as much as the next kid, but riding a motorcycle was way more exciting than throwing a baseball for me. During high school I got very serious with riding dirt bikes and began traveling across California to compete in races. By college, most of my attention had been directed at studying business and stunt riding. My two passions had become riding and business, so I decided to combine the two of them.

So here I am, twenty years later, on my way to my first oversees performance, preparing myself for a weekend in paradise.

I was surrounded by seven beautiful girls on an international flight. The girls and I were hired by Hot Import Nights to perform in Guam for an import car show. I was hired to perform stunts on a motorcycle and the girls would model, go-go dance, and DJ the event. The thirteen hour flight to Guam wouldn't be so bad with these ladies. Karen was tall, about 5'11", and with the long blonde hair she reminded me of a super model. Jeni was only five feet, but she was gorgeous. Sabina was Persian and slender with long, gorgeous legs, while Nicky was petite with a face of such natural beauty that it made the girl next door jealous. I mean, seriously, I couldn't have thought up a better group of girls to travel with.

After we landed, grabbed our bags, and got our passports stamped, we met up with another member of our group, the Drifter Kid. No, he wasn't a vagabond, but a drifter like the kind you would find in, The Fast and the Furious. Like me, he would showcase his skills at the event. When DJ Lisa and Ursula joined the group we jumped in the limo and were off to the hotel.

The hotel was oceanfront paradise; we arrived after night had already fallen. Needless to say it didn't take much time to get from the hotel to the water, which was more or less a stone's throw away. Guam fit the bill for that picture-perfect tropical getaway.

The girls were leading the charge down to the beach in the moonlight. When girls like that were leading me to water, it didn't matter that I didn't have swim trunks for the occasion. Boxer shorts for me and underwear for the girls. The trip was off to a "rough" start.

When it came time for settling in, I roomed with an editor of Import Car Magazine named Stew, a very nice Canadian who came down to cover the event.

The next morning we headed straight to the beach to take advantage of the beautiful scenery and relax. The later hours of the day would consist of interviews with the paper and local radio show, but the morning hours were ours. I should have partaken in a nutrient-filled breakfast with the hopes of recovering after a fourteen-hour plane ride, which can be quite taxing on the body. Instead, I went to the bar and ordered a couple beers, figuring a light buzz would do just that.

As Drifter Kid and the models emerged from the hotel, every head in the place turned. Emily decided to utilize the majestic scenery for her own personal photo shoot. It wasn't professional, mind you, but when you are that attractive, it doesn't matter that you're shooting with a windup camera you purchased at the local drug store, heads are still going to turn. I'll admit I was also enchanted by these sirens' spell; it was hard to turn away as my mind joined the collective male consciousness on the beach.

That afternoon we did our best to work through the press

interviews. I gave my speech about what it is I do for a living, talking points that I know the general public would find interesting.

After the interview, things got kind of hazy. We'd been in the sun all day and were sleep-deprived. Thus, we had the brilliant notion to keep drinking. Luckily for us, our inebriated state didn't affect the locals' kindness towards us as we went to the neighborhood dive. I'm sure it had nothing to do with the seven beautiful girls we were with.

Regardless, we were given free drinks and served great food. The bartender allowed the girls to dance on the tables and pour shots for the locals. It was crazy but civil at the same time, if that makes sense. The locals on Guam had an air of cool about them. Don't get me wrong, they were excited to have the girls dancing and pouring booze down their throats, but they were respectful. At that point, the Guam culture started standing out to me. It wasn't something that I could put my finger on; it was a kind of old-school mentality.

Of course, that sort of thinking didn't exactly apply to the group I came over here with, which adhered to the idea that drinking isn't a marathon but rather a race. These girls had it in their head that they could keep up with me drink-for-drink. And when you are my size, 6'0" and one-hundred and ninety-five pounds, the concept of keeping up, generally doesn't work out too well. I wanted to relax not play drinking games.

I've never been much of a dancer, but that night I was feeling great and got my butt on the dance floor. I worked my way over to one of the beautiful models, Karen. She was the tall blonde with legs that went all the way up and had curves for days. She must have noticed me checking her out as she proceeded to grab my hands and hold them over her body. She reached around the back of my neck, pulled me further into her and kissed me.

Finally, for whatever reason, she proceeded to tell me how lucky I was since she had a boyfriend back home. Me being me, I pulled her close, put my mouth to her ear and said,

"Lucky guy."

Yup. That killed it, and she danced over to the bar and left me and my big mouth alone for the rest of the night.

The next day was all business. I definitely felt the repercussions of the night before. I finally got some food and washed it down quickly as I was anxious to check out the bike I would be riding for the show. The thing about performing overseas is that it's quite costly to import, which meant rather than riding my own bike for the show, the promoter paid a local biker to lend me his motorcycle for the event. My sponsors wanted to make sure they got their parts on the motorcycle so they shipped everything to the local motorcycle shop for installation. The local shop had most of the bike tricked out, when I checked in with them and assured me it would be ready in time for the performance.

Seeing that the bike was being taken care of, I headed over to the event center to get a feel for the drag strip on which I was going to perform. I don't always have this opportunity, but if I can, I like to check out where I will be performing before it gets crowded and the excitement hits the air. I like to sit back and take it all in. I try to keep that little piece of imagery in my mind, the emptiness, the calm before the storm.

This is part of the preparedness I carry with me from my younger years at the track with my father. When I practice, I stick to a few places—secret spots, if you will—usually large, empty parking lots. These practice areas have an emptiness that provides a comfort, a familiarity, if that makes sense. I mean, every place I go is different, but that emptiness when no one else is around, that is the same. I guess that familiarity that exists in my mind when the crowd fills the bleachers and loud music fills the air, always exists in the background. Don't get me wrong, I get excited from the crowd—but the lot becomes my canvas to shine.

After checking out the drag strip, I wanted to relax, take my mind off things. I spent the remainder of the day wandering around Guam with Drifter Kid. We made friends with a few locals and they were kind enough to show us around. We ended up at our local bar again. We cracked open a few beers and the locals gave us a brief history lesson of Guam.

While Drifter Kid and I were chatting things up, the room fell silent. Emily walked into the bar, ordered a beer, and sat down next to us without speaking a word. The mere presence of her got us in the mood to keep drinking.

The thing about pretty girls is once you set one in motion, they attract others. Hours later, it was like *déjà vu*, girls dancing and drinking all over again. It was fun for a while until we came up with the idea to try out the hotel pool and water slide. Needless to say, it took all of about one minute for us to pile in the van and we were gone.

Drifter Kid and I changed and were down at the pool in 5 minutes flat. We dove into that water so fast… man, nothing beats a good buzz, warm weather, and some cool water.

Drifter and I had brought a surplus of cold beer to the pool and after a while began to wonder what was taking the ladies so long. Then bottles in hands, mouths wide open… we saw four of the most stunning women on the island walking our way in bikinis.

What is better than beautiful girls, adult beverages, and a pool on the beach? That evening's lineup consisted of the following:

Sabina, do I really need to say more with such an exotic name? And there was Karen, blonde and beautiful; Jeni a petite Asian with incredible physique; Nicky, a half-Mexican girl that could light up the room.

So there we were in the middle of the night, drinking and carrying on like you would with four girls in paradise. I couldn't help but wonder why the security guards weren't throwing us out.

"Come on, Clint," I said to myself. "These guys are having as much fun watching the girls play as you are…"

Well, not quite as much.

The fun can only last so long, and the morning finally arrived— the proverbial "game day," if you will. It was time for me to do what I do best: perform and entertain. The morning couldn't have started off better: a good breakfast followed by a light jog down the beach. My head was clear and I was pumped. I was going to show this island some sportbike freestyle.

We were off to a good start as the promoter picked us up in style. It was a limo bus, tricked out all the way: plasma TV, stripper pole, and loaded with booze. Passengers included Drifter Kid, the models, Stew, and a handful of Japanese magazine writers hired to cover the event.

Hot Import Nights are geared to do several things including overloading all your senses in one evening. We pulled in and hundreds of beautiful custom cars were lined up, tons of people having a good time, and in store for even a better one once we did our thing. I could feel the energy before I stepped out of the limo.

The music and atmosphere gave a lively pulse that thudded in the background as Drifter and I hatched a plan of attack in our dressing room. The venue had it laid out that the kid and I were going to perform at different times, but we wanted to pull off a big finish with a side-by-side performance, Drifter doing his thing in his car and me busting wheelies around him. He smirked and I gave him a nod; it was going to be epic and we both knew it.

The dressing room was located on the second floor of an office toward the side of the track. I walked out on to the balcony and leaned against the metal poll railing, posting up, taking it all in. The drag strip had transformed from yesterday; that emptiness was gone, consumed by a sea of energy that I had come here to let explode. And to think, my high school guidance counselor had advised me to get a desk job with benefits. That man had no imagination. Funny how that works.

The Drifter was up first. Much like my situation, the kid had borrowed a car from one of the locals. He turned the key and sped off. In no time, the air reeked with that sweet smell of burned rubber, and the kid had that car drifting all over the drag strip, the turbo whistling as he slammed the gas down, breaking the rear end loose. The place was erupting and I could feel the adrenaline coursing through my veins.

The crowd was on their feet as this 22-year-old kid was showing them what it meant to drive the wheels off. Maybe it was fate or that the local's car had never been driven that hard before, but it suddenly made a loud noise that sounded like a gun shot. And when you hear a noise like that, it can't be good. The car puttered to a slow stop and the kid climbed out. He shook his head and started walking toward the side of the track. He was done for the night after only fifteen minutes of performing.

I could tell he was disappointed. He had come here to go big and he had come up short. I patted him on the shoulder. He stomached the disappointment well, but I knew having the car quit on him like that had to hurt. I knew I had to come up big, not just for me, but for him too.

Rather than preplanning what stunts I was going to do, I tried to get a feel for the crowd and what they wanted to see. Since I was in Guam and seeing all the energy the crowd had just given the Kid, I wasn't about to let these folks down.

When was I ever going to get this opportunity again?

I figured I'd start off with a basic wheelie and work my way up from there. I put on my helmet and took a deep breath. This wasn't my bike, but it looked like the shop had done a good job putting on all of my sponsor's parts, so it wasn't like I was sitting on a complete stranger.

So I hit the throttle and came out strong, popping up the front wheel. The bike felt a bit heavy, but the throttle was responsive, putting out more than enough power to compensate.

It's funny the nuances one considers as you progress in your profession, those little things that make the slightest difference. But one thing, regardless of your level of expertise, is having good brakes.

With a slight groan in my head I realized I didn't have rear brakes. And when you don't have rear brakes, it's very difficult, almost impossible, to perform.

The way I saw it was I had two options: I could hang it up and call it a day, or, I could man up. And with a crowd like that, and considering what had happened to the kid's car, I wasn't about to put on the brake on my performance. Frustrating as this was, I still tried to bust out some stunts that didn't require me utilizing the rear brake, such as standing on the top of the tank and acrobatic moves. Thing was, the best I was able to perform wasn't good. I'm human, just like everyone else, and despite my efforts to keep going, for the first time in my life, I felt completely impotent.

My last trick was sorry and I knew it. I tossed the bike on the ground, threw up my hands and walked away. There was only so much I could do. I'm here in the middle of the Philippine Sea trying to put on a bad-ass show with no rear brakes. I am used to performing at a certain level, and when that level was not up to par, I began to feel badly for the spectators. Drifter Kid and I both felt like shit.

We'd come to perform, and hadn't. When you get to this level, you can't blame it on your bike. These people came to be entertained. And honestly, at the end of the day it was my fault because I knew better. Hell, I'd been raised better. It was a nagging guilt, the guilt of my father pulling his hat down, shaking his head, and saying, "Shit." I should have gone over that bike myself just like my dad had taught me to do since I was young. More than anything, I wanted to blame the bike shop. I wanted to get in their face and yell,

"How could you have not checked the brakes!?"

But I knew my mind was just attempting to place the blame elsewhere. I screwed up, and it hurt; my pride just didn't want to acknowledge it. I didn't want this feeling and hadn't prepared for it. I needed a beer, and I needed to sulk. I needed some perspective.

While the situation sucked, I have very real expectations about myself and my profession: if you get up more than you fall, you'll be alright. It might hurt a little, but you'll survive. And while my current mood definitely sucked and I should have known better than to sulk.

Things weren't that bad. I tilted my head back, and took a long pull. The beer tasted damn good.

With one sip down and number two ready to go, the event coordinator pulled me aside. He was yelling something in my ear and I was shaking my head because I didn't think I heard him right. "Are you serious?"

The coordinator and I walked behind to the staging area and the coordinator nodded his head towards a guy standing off to the side.

We shook hands and the guy reaffirmed what I thought the coordinator had shouted in my ear moments ago. Like I said, if you get up more than you fall, you'll be okay. The guy back stage was a spectator. He'd watched my show, saw what happened, and he said to me,

"How would you like to use my bike for the show?"

I was still in disbelief. He cocked his thumb over his shoulder, pointing to a brand new Suzuki GSXR 1000.

"So, what do you say?"

My mind was saying yes but my mind's internal governor was holding me back. Did this guy know what I do for a living?

Didn't he just see me tear through that last bike and throw it on the ground? I mean, stunting is just a polite way of saying I bust up motorcycles for a living. Remember when I said they have this old-school mentality on the island? Well, I'll be damned if he didn't say that it would be an honor for me to perform on his motorcycle.

I looked him square in the eyes, and we shook hands. Needless to say, we both understood that the honor was all mine. But I couldn't help myself.

"I might bring your bike back with a few missing pieces,"

I said to him after giving it a once over. This was a ten-thousand dollar bike. I didn't want to give him any misconceptions about what was going to happen. When he didn't respond, I looked over my shoulder. He was standing there with his arms folded and smiling. I could feel that adrenaline pumping through my veins. This was redemption!

Smoke billowed from the back tire as I burned out and drifted across the drag strip. The crowd was roaring and I was busting wheelies up and down the track. I was able to handle the bike really well; it had a good balance and was responsive. More importantly, the brakes worked and so far I was able to perform for twenty minutes without damaging it. But it was nearing ten p.m. and these people came to see a good show; I didn't want them sitting in their seats when I was done. I wanted them standing. I wanted to give them something to talk about that would bring them back next year. What I wanted to do wasn't the most technical of tricks, but judging by the atmosphere, it would be the most memorable, and it wouldn't destroy this bike.

I rounded toward the end of the track and then pinned it; the bike and I took off like a rocket. My heart was racing and I could feel my palms sweating in my gloves. The sound of the engine let me know when it was time. I was nearly in front of the stands, the time was now. I popped the clutch and pulled the front wheel up not just hard, but as hard as I could. The front wheel was spinning, rising straight up towards the moon with the exhaust pipe heading south, grinding against the concrete, spewing a trail of sparks behind me into the night as I went roaring by the length of the grandstands.

I brought the bike down and as the front wheel connected with the asphalt, a calming, cold numbness surged through my body. For a second, I didn't really remember hearing much of anything, not the crowd, not the bike, not even my own heart; only a solitary breath that escaped from my lungs. I couldn't help but smile. I was stoked and raised my hands in the air as I headed back to the grandstand. I wish I could have told the crowd how good that just felt. That I felt terrible about my previous performance and really wanted to prove to them what I could do. But it looked like they already knew. They were on their feet, cheering and yelling. It was electric.

Not to sound cliché, but all the hours of practice and determination to get to that point had paid off.

I rode toward the back of the staging area where the owner of the bike and his wife were waiting. They were grinning ear to ear, his wife waving a hand-held video camera, urging me to come forward so we could watch the footage she had captured. I tossed him the keys and thanked him. To return the favor, I gave the guy my new helmet. Without this guy stepping up, I would have been drinking to forget rather than to celebrate.

We parted ways and with a cold beer in hand, Drifter Kid and I headed over to see if the girls were having better luck.

We posted up near the side of the stage where DJ Lisa was putting on a show for the crowd bumping her music while Karen, Nicky, Jeni, and Sabina were dancing for the crowd. Off to the right of the stage Emily and Ursula were signing autograph posters for their fans. It was great to see the crowd dancing and partying the night away.

The next day the sun was bright and a warm breeze swept across the beach. I was hoping to spend my last day in Guam relaxing.

Beach all morning and then off to a birthday party that afternoon. One of the bouncers had invited us to his birthday party, and if the rumors were true about how good his family's food was, there was no way I was going to pass up that invitation.

I hiked down the beach and plunged into the water. I lay floating on my back, looking up towards the sky. Did I really want to keep my office job? Maybe I could do this full time?

The problem with being surrounded by beautiful girls on a tropical beach while drinking margaritas is that time stands still. But it keeps on running for the rest of the world, and before we realized it, morning had turned into afternoon, four thirty to be exact. The bouncer's birthday party started at four. We were late!

To make matters worse, trying to get seven women ready to go out for the night is like watching paint dry. No matter how much you want to scream and yell, they are going to take their sweet time. Four thirty turned into five, and we finally made it to the party by five thirty. So, relatively speaking, for being on the beach all day while drinking, an hour turn-around time in "girl time" wasn't too bad. Still, I like to be on time, so it didn't bode well with me.

As we walked into the bar my stomach sank. And no, not because I was starving or that it was filled full of tropical, sugary booze; it sank because all the food that had been laid out on the tables was still there; it was covered and uneaten.

We walked in and you could hear a pin drop; it was that quiet.

It turned out, the old-school style that exists only in movies, was alive and well in Guam. We said we would show up at four thirty and they had taken us at our word. This wasn't L.A. arriving fashionably late or make a promise to show up only to cancel later. No, Guam was old-school mentality, and it made me feel terrible regardless of the excuses. But this was Guam, the island and its people took us in with open arms and that moment of silence, the uncomfortable feeling, vanished as quickly as it arrived.

The food couldn't have been better. I ate and drank until I couldn't pack it in anymore. The conversation was light, and pleasant, mostly about how our stay had been and about the performance last night. After we ate, the girls, Drifter Kid, and I all danced. Before we knew it, it was late and the bar was closing. But we weren't ready to call it a night. A group of girls and guys from the party wanted to head over to the local strip club and have some more drinks. Of course, we decided to join them.

Now, I'm not sure if it was the fact that I was spoiled considering my current company, but these strippers didn't have any business taking off their clothes for a living. Needless to say, it took all of about five minutes before we decided to leave.

We only had the limo for another hour, which was just as well because at the rate we were drinking, there would be nothing left in the limo bar anyway. I remember reaching for a bottle of vodka and rather than mixing it with coke or orange juice, I poured it straight down the hatch, passed it around, and before I knew it, another bottle was done.

By the time the limo dropped us off it was around three in the morning. I was hammered, but one of the girls was way worse off. So there I was, helping her through the lobby of our hotel and she decided to stop. I knew this wasn't good. She let go of my hand, popped a squat and screamed,

"I can't hold it anymore!"

Urine pooled around her legs and over the marble floor.

I doubted that the security guards that had enjoyed watching us at the pool would find this stunt as amusing. I was seeing double by this point, and it took every bit of my concentration to help get her safely up stairs with the other girls.

I put her to bed and sat on the couch, glad to be off my feet so the world could stabilize a bit. The other girls piled in the room and while they were drunk, they were not ready to call it quits.

"Let's play a drinking game!" they announced.

Now, the last time I played a drinking game was in college. It involved a shot glass, a quarter, a wooden table, and a pack of less than attractive girls. For whatever reason, that memory resonated in my head, and while I don't really care for drinking games, I didn't want to be a stick in the mud. At least here, the girls were pretty.

Bounce... bounce... bounce. That was how it went with quarter and the shot glass. I think I was like zero for ten at that point, which wasn't bad because I was having trouble keeping my eyes open, and my speech was starting to be less than intelligible. Besides, it was nearing four and that seven-in-the-morning flight was nearing. My body was shutting down; it needed sleep.

I can't remember what they were saying as I left their room, but I mumbled something about what a good time I had had and how I'd see them all in a few hours. I made it to my room and I was out...

"Clint! Wake up, man!"

I was shaking my head with one of the worst hangovers ever. I told Stew, my Canadian roommate, to keep it down, but he kept going on and on about getting my stuff together so that I can catch my flight. I seriously felt like sleeping another two days at least. I sat up and besides the world doing a little spin, something else was seriously wrong. My shirt was pulled up around my arms, my pants were completely off, my boxers were halfway down my thighs, and I reeked of Lubriderm. I looked at Stew and he quickly looked away, busying himself with packing.

"Stew, what the hell is going on?"

"Come on, man. I've been yelling at you to get up for the past five minutes. We don't have time for this."

"Like hell we don't," I said.

"I'm not going anywhere until you explain this shit."

Stew sat on his bed and let out a deep sigh.

"I told them to stop..." he said trailing off.

Oh, shit. This wasn't good.

Apparently, I had locked Stew out of the room, and I was so drunk that I hadn't heard him pounding on the door. He had gone to the lobby to get another key at four in the morning, come back upstairs, and as it turns out four of the girls weren't ready to call it a night. They spied him in the hall and were on him like jackals, wanting to see what was going on in Clint's room. Stew was helpless but to let them in… and that's when things got weird.

Images started flashing in my mind and as Stew told me the story, the blank spaces started to fill in. Jesus. The girls had attacked me in full force, while apparently I was mumbling nonsensical things at that point, but that didn't discourage their efforts. Stew told them to stop but his efforts were useless. He might as well have curled up in the fetal position in the corner of the room.

Stew looked down at his watch. "I have got to run, man. I was supposed to be at the airport twenty minutes ago; I have work tomorrow."

"Stew? What happened? You can't leave me hanging like this."

"Sorry, man."

He grabbed his gear and was out the door, and yet again, I felt like I had been royally screwed. I mean, it's not every day you wake up with your pants down around your ankles with junk smelling like Lubriderm.

But Stew was right; I also had a flight to catch.

Only God knows how, but I packed up my stuff and made it to the airport bus with everyone. The previous night, these girls were gorgeous. But this morning, they have no make-up, their hair is unkempt, and they are smoking cigarettes. Basically, several notches below stripper hot. I don't care who you are, after a night of drinking like that… beauty is hard to come by. I guess the only time girls won't take endless hours to get ready is after a hard night of drinking and before a fourteen-hour flight home, back to the States.

Not that I was looking like a prince by any means, but I had that internal fire kindling in my stomach. They had played with me while I was sleeping, and I wanted to figure out what the hell had happened. I'm sure the fact that I was still drunk only encouraged my efforts to get to the bottom of this, and I knew just how I was going to do it.

A fourteen-hour plane flight is long, and the flight is even longer if you have an itch you can't scratch or a secret you just can't keep. So I cornered Sabina about midway through the flight, just about the time when she would have been settling in, perhaps getting a little comfortable with her surroundings, and glad to get a little shut eye. But not that day, not until she explained what went down in the wee hours of this morning. Maybe it was the hangover, the guilt, the hair of the dog, or the mere fact she just wanted to be left alone for the remainder of the flight that led to her confession.

What she told me is the stuff that guys wish happened, things you see in porno movies, and I'm pretty sure if the shoe was on the other foot, meaning one passed out girl and four guys, this story would have a completely different ending. From what she had told me thus far, her and Stew's story matched up, but when she tried to leave it at that, I pressed her. I wanted to know about the Lubriderm.

"What the hell happened? Why don't I remember anything from last night?" I pointed to my crotch not realizing my voice was starting to get a little loud. She told me to keep my voice down, looked away, then down at my crotch, and smiled.

"You weren't that drunk."

"But I was passed out..." I said.

"Clint..." she said. Her head was down, her hands working into her palms. "We... must have... must have messed around with you for a good hour but we all got tired and passed out."

The plane landed in LAX, and I hiked over to my truck that had been parked on the second floor of the garage for the past week. As I was throwing my luggage in the back, I heard two voices come from behind me. Well, if it wasn't molester number one and number two. They needed a ride home and were wondering if I could help. I wasn't in the mood to do them any favors but I also didn't want to be huge jerk and leave them stranded. Karen told me which exit to take so I flipped on the blinker. I drove through a few neighborhood streets and she pointed to her house. As I put my truck in park and they start getting out, this big dude started heading in our direction.

"Oh, do you know that guy?"

I asked, knowing my moment has come.

Karen gave me an awkward smile.

"Yeah, that's my boyfriend."

A grin reaches my ears as I muttered, "Lucky guy."

It was this trip I realized stunt riding was not just a sport, it was a lifestyle for me.

2 YOUNG EWING

I grew up in Santa Barbara, California—specifically, Montecito, an upscale part of Santa Barbara. My parents both worked, in order to provide a good education for my brother and I. As far back as I can remember, we were given chores in and outside of the house. I thought that every kid in America did chores, until I started wising up to the fact that a lot of parents didn't ask their kids to do anything. Most notably, at around 4th grade, I noticed that other kids from the neighborhood would be playing all day with little to no chores. For my brother and I it was a different story. Before we could do anything, we had to be outside pulling weeds, taking out the trash, mowing the lawn, or helping our dad take stuff to the dump. As a kid, I couldn't wait to be finished with these duties, but as I got older I realized how much these responsibilities shaped my brother and I for the future. I think it's fair to say that, as I got older, I began to truly understand and appreciate how my parents treated us.

As I got into dirt bikes at a young age, I began to work more around the house, in order to pay for practices, races, and parts for the motorcycle. My dad would split up his weekend, taking my brother to football games and me to the racetrack to ride. I was fortunate to have a father that would give up his free time in order to make his kids happy.

By the time I entered 6th grade, baseball had become too slow for me and football was of no interest because it was a team sport. Racing dirt bikes was an individual sport, where it was easily measured who came in first. I loved the fact that I was in charge of how fast and how big I could make the motorcycle go. I didn't have a driver's license at age 12, but I could jump a dirt bike 50 feet!

When I entered Bishop Diego, a private Catholic high school in Santa Barbara, most of the other kids had nice cars. Actually, most of the kids in Montecito had really nice cars—but my first car didn't even run. In fact, my dad and I towed my Honda into Montecito. I think you could say with confidence that, to this day, it has probably been the only car towed into Montecito rather than out. My dad brought the car home in order to show me how to work on it and ultimately, to learn to appreciate it.

By my sophomore year, my parents were splitting up and I began to feel like I was floating through life.

My brother was off in college, and I didn't have the anchor I once had. I began splitting my time between parents, which meant I was in charge of myself a lot of the time. I would say that the two things that kept me on track were riding and my best friend. I trained down at the local boxing club, which kept me busy after school, and practicing riding and racing kept me busy on the weekends, so that left me with very little time to find trouble. I was drinking a lot and going to a lot of parties during my downtime, and it felt like I was getting an early jump on college—or at least, with the party aspect of it.

Most of my brothers' friends were now going to UCSB and throwing some big parties—and with UCSB just miles from my high school; this meant that my friends and I found ourselves out at college parties often. I wouldn't say I was out of control, because I had a part time job and was still racing and going to school—but I was only good at one of them, and let's just say, it wasn't riding or school. I was consistently placing in the top three during races, but I wasn't first, and with school I wasn't flunking, but I was only holding a C average. I was only 16, but I was acting like I was 22. The parties, concerts, racing, and not having a permanent home was a recipe for disaster.

Then one day in school, it hit me:

Was I going to live my life like this forever?

Was I going to go through life being average?

My mom and dad didn't teach me to be average and didn't work as hard as they did so that I could go to private school and get C's. This was not who I wanted to be, and I was going to change it as quickly as I could. I wasn't blaming my parents for breaking up. I wanted them to both be happy with their lives so that I could also focus on how to be happy again.

As it turns out, raising your Grade Point Average back up is a lot harder when you spend two years not caring. I had to refocus my life and teach myself how to study again.

With help from my friend's mom, Mrs. Sampas, I was steered in the right direction to get myself back on track and into college. That summer she insisted I enroll myself in a college-level course at the local junior college, in order to get the jump on my junior and senior years. It was going to take a lot of studying and some high test scores to raise my overall GPA. By mid-junior year, I was back on track and doing well, but raising my GPA was a lot harder than I had anticipated.

My teachers were starting to notice a difference, and one day my history teacher asked me to stay after class to speak to her. She told me that my grades were getting better as the weeks progressed and she hoped I would keep it up. I was getting closer to an A on her weekly test, but still the best I had done was a B+. I told her that on the upcoming test I would do my best for that A. Then she said something I will never forget.

She said if I scored a 90% or better she would personally drive over to my favorite burger joint in town and get me a burger, fries, and a shake for lunch. GAME ON, I told her, and the deal was made.

That week I was nose deep in my book—but it wasn't the free hamburger that was my incentive to do well, it was the fact that she had noticed me trying and cared enough to say something. That Friday I took the test and felt that it went well. My next period was Spanish, and all I could think about was the score on my history test. After Spanish was lunch, and with my teacher not in sight, I thought to myself that I had not reached my goal.

But fifteen minutes into my lunch period, I saw my history teacher walking over to me. She had a bag in one hand and what looked like a drink in the other. She walked up to me and congratulated me on my 91%. That was another turning point for me in high school but also in life. Not only had I learned that could I do what I set my mind to in school and with education, but I also had learned that some people notice and care.

By senior year, I was doing my very best to bring my grades up and keep my nose clean. That is why hearing my name called over the PA system came as a shock. The Dean of Students, Mr. Ward, was calling me into his office. Walking from class I began to feel a bit worried, since this was the dean of disciplinary action. But what was I worrying about? I sat down in his office and after a period of silence, he turned his computer around to face me and asked me a simple question:

"Do you notice anything strange on this computer screen?"

It looked as though he was looking at my grade records from freshman to senior year. Off the top of my head, I didn't notice anything unusual. He then asked, "What happened?"

Excuse me?

I didn't understand his question.

What happened to what?

"What happened in your life, Clint, from you getting D's and C's to now getting B's and a few A's?"

The answer was simple: I wanted more out of myself than to be average. Going home that day, I was still shocked that he had even noticed. It seemed that this high school staff did in fact care about their students and took note of their accomplishments, whether that student was the valedictorian or just the average student not looking to be average anymore.

In my senior year, I sold my dirt bike and purchased a street bike. My parents were very surprised, but I didn't see myself turning pro while also trying to go to college. For me, it was important to get my education, especially since I had already had my share of injuries from dirt bike riding. By my senior year of high school, I had already broken both hands, a plate in my right foot, and my shoulder. I knew that I didn't want to stay in town, but instead wanted a college experience outside of Santa Barbara. Fortunately, by that time, my grades were high enough for me to be accepted into Sonoma State University.

Mrs. Sampas had given me the guidance and discipline necessary to further myself with a college education. It was a good thing she had, because it made the transition from high school to college possible and much smoother. I knew how to study but also to relax and enjoy college.

After a few months, however, I realized that I was missing the thrill of riding dirt bikes. For me the dirt bike was a way to work my energy out and to get a great dose of adrenaline. Now instead of racing on the track, I was going to classes and riding my street bike.

I would describe my freshman year as anything but typical. To me, school was okay, but I didn't have a way to get my energy out. From once having a regular adrenaline outlet, I was now tied down with books and studying.

I remember riding my street bike to class one day and thinking about what would happen if I started riding my street bike like a dirt bike. I began to try some wheelies and burnouts. I wasn't racing around town but had chosen a private parking lot to practice my skills. It was the adrenaline rush I needed, and it felt nice to be doing something very similar to my dirt bike days. I quickly got the hang of it, so I started challenging myself with how long I could carry a wheelie. I began watching videos about guys stunting on sportbikes and it quickly sparked further interest into how far I could take this interest.

I got a job at a local motorcycle shop and soon became known as a pretty good rider. I was by no means a fast rider on the road or track, but I could get my bike to maneuver any which way. One day, the best stunt rider in northern California stopped by the shop and asked for me by name. When I met him, he told me he had heard I was pretty good at riding wheelies and challenged me to see who could ride the longest wheelie.

Later that week, we met up and set out on Highway 101 in Santa Rosa, California. There is a nice 5 mile stretch of highway on that road with virtually no bend. As we entered the freeway, we paired our mph and brought the front wheels up to start the challenge. From the first moment I saw him wheelie, I could see that he had a different style from mine. He was using more of his rear brake, and I was using more balance. After two miles or so of riding this wheelie, I began to get tired from holding on, but just as I thought I couldn't hold on any longer, the other rider brought his wheel down first. As it turned out, his different riding style was one that I soon adapted to. He may have lost that challenge, but in order for me to improve my technique, his style of using his brakes would be the future of riding for me.

After that challenge, we became good friends, and he began to show me the ropes of how to slow down my wheelies and become a bit more technical with them. I began practicing more when I had the time, but for me graduating was the most important goal. In 2003, sportbike freestyle riding was in its infancy, and so was my career after college. I had just gotten my first job after college, selling ad space in newspapers, but at the same time I was beginning to excel at riding.

In 2004, I landed my first show for a local shop, and I started to think that perhaps riding was something I could start doing on the side, picking up small stunt shows for motorcycle shops within California.

By 2006, I was busy performing with another rider at car shows, motorcycle shops, and even an AMA superbike race. I was busy riding and traveling on the weekends and working my normal job during the week. It even came to the point where my friend would drive my bike to out-of-state shows and I would fly out to join him on Friday after work. It was a balancing act that was keeping me very busy.

I realized that I was being torn between riding and work, and I was not giving my all to either. My friend kept telling me to stop working and start riding full time, but financially this was not feasible, as we were only doing about 14 shows a year. What set my friend and I apart from most riders at the time was the fact that we would try to perform at the largest venues or events we could find. We were booking races, monster truck shows, and even Indy car. We wanted to make a career of sportbike freestyle riding. The only problem was that, at the time, nobody was riding full time. Then we stopped seeing this as a problem and instead looked at it as an opportunity to be the first. There was no handbook or tutorial about riding full time. There wasn't even someone to learn from. We were learning something new with each show, each sponsor, and each year.

By 2007, I was determined to become one of the first riders in California to go pro as a professional rider. The marketing skills I learned in college would need to start playing more of a role with my riding. I needed to set myself apart from other riders, not only with my riding ability but also with my brand identity. I needed to create CLINT EWING.

3 15 MINUTES OF FAME

The year 2007 was a big year for my career as a professional sportbike freestyle rider. During that year, I was juggling a full-time job selling used Cisco equipment, performing stunt shows on the weekends, and taking my first trip overseas to perform. In the summer of 2007, I received news that I would be sponsored by the largest motorcycle parts distributor and tire Company. I would also have the chance to attempt my first Guinness World Record on national TV. This year would be better known as my breakout year!

Early in the year, I was contacted by the CEO of my apparel sponsor, who told me that he was branching out and launching a new motorcycle apparel company. He asked if I would spearhead the company's promotional campaign as the new face of freestyle riding. I will never forget Bruce flying to California to offer me a position as a professional athlete representing Speed & Strength. We went out to dinner and discussed the details of what would be asked of me as the company's rider. I did not take this meeting lightly, as I had put in a lot of hard work traveling, performing, marketing myself, and even crashing to get to this position. As one might imagine, there is no guidebook on how to become a professional "freestyle rider."

I busted my ass to get to this point in my career and life. I worked hard for my bachelors degree and existing sponsors. It was the combination of the businessman and athlete that got me to this point. The businessman in me is the silent partner, the man that works behind closed doors and sets goals six months to a year ahead of time. I only take a moment to mention this because it is difficult for many to realize that yes, there is fun to be had with riding professionally. But there is also a ton of work behind the scenes that most don't know about or care to see. This was a unique trade that I was constantly learning.

By the end of the meeting with Bruce, I was excited about the opportunities ahead and the chance to show him that I could live up to his expectations and excel. It was official! I was the first freestyle athlete of the Speed & Strength brand.

Two months later, I received a call from Dunlop Tires. They had received a recommendation from one of my current sponsors and wanted to offer me an opportunity to represent their brand.

By 2007, stunt riding had gained in popularity not only within the motorcycle culture but also within the motorsports community as a whole. Races were featuring stunt shows as the halftime entertainment, there were magazines specifically catering to the culture of stunt riding, and there was even a TV show about stunt riding.

With a combination of hard work and great timing, I had recently achieved all three areas of exposure. A few of my performances had recently been covered in sportbike magazines, I had made my first appearance on TV, and I had just completed one of my largest shows at the AMA superbike races in California.

After 20 minutes on the phone and an outline of what was expected of me, I was informed that I would receive a formal contract in the mail and that I would now be representing the Dunlop brand. I remember thinking that this was one of the best days of my life for two reasons: the honor of becoming a rider for such a respected brand, and the fact that I no longer had to buy three tires a month!

Now it was officially my job to burn through tires! Sure enough, a few days later I received my contract in the mail as well as my first allotment of tires.

With my year off to a great start, I was also doing well with the number of events I was performing in throughout the year. Normally, 10-15 shows were a great number for me, but in 2007 I had 23 shows, including a trip to Guam. I had a lot of motivation to do well, with two new sponsors on board, and I wanted to show them I could be a great asset.

I was also at crossroads in my life; should I focus on a career in sales or take the risk and go for the glory riding full time?

What kind of career could I have as a professional stunt rider, compared to the security of bringing home good money every two weeks from my office job? After a few months of contemplating, I received a call that would make my decision that much easier.

That November I received a call from my new manager, who told me that NBC was interested in having me attempt a Guinness World Record on live TV. I was at work when I received the phone call, and from that day forward, work was never the same.

Later that evening, my manager began to fill me in on the details of the stunt. I was being asked to attempt to beat the Guinness World Record for longest ride through a tunnel of fire on a motorcycle! I would have to navigate through a tunnel of fire that was 6 feet tall, 10 feet wide, and 200 feet long. I was informed that there had been an attempt in England the year before, but that the rider didn't make it all the way through. He had punched out the side of the tunnel and had broken his collarbone. My first thought should have been fear, but instead it was a level of excitement at the chance to accomplish such a feat. Was this something I had ever done before—or even thought of? No, I'm a freestyle rider, not a tunnel of fire guy!

But on the other hand, it was national exposure and a great way to kick off 2008 with my sponsors.

After thinking it over that night, I broke it down into a simple question for myself: Do I decline the offer and keep doing what I am currently doing, or do I want to take the risk and see what this opportunity will blossom into?

The next day I called my manager and informed him I was willing to risk it and go for the record. A few weeks later I signed the paperwork and the date was set for January 2008 for a live two-hour Guinness World Record special on NBC.

I shared the news with my sponsors, and they seemed excited for the exposure and for my career. Needless to say, my parents weren't thrilled—and they cautioned me as to the obvious dangers if things went wrong. It's not the easiest thing, to explain to your parents that you will be risking your life because it's a challenge and will further your career.

My mother always reminds me that there's a reason I went to college to get a degree. I saw college as the opportunity to leave Santa Barbara and focus on bettering myself with education. This is not to say that I knew exactly what I wanted to do with myself. In fact, for as long I could remember, I never knew what I wanted to do with my life or for a living. I just knew that a college education would be a step in the right direction. I wanted to be happy and to enjoy what I did. That may seem like an obvious position for most, but at some point in our lives we may find ourselves rationalizing other choices, until we end up at a place in life that we never thought we would be, emotionally and physically.

Most people thought I was plain crazy when I explained to them what I was going for. It really just comes down to the kind of person I am. When I first started out riding dirt bikes at age 8, my father would take me to the motocross track, and I would practice from morning to night. As I progressed, my jumps got bigger and my speeds got faster, and before long I wanted to be able to clear every jump and accomplish every obstacle on the track. I was by no means going to be a professional motocross rider, but I at least wanted to try the biggest and scariest jumps the professionals were doing. If I went to a new track and chickened out on the largest jump, it would ruin my day. So the first thing I had to do when arriving was to hit the largest jump there. Why couldn't I just relax and have fun like most other people? I'm still trying to figure that out. This tunnel was in all respects just another jump I had to accomplish, except that this time it was a 200-foot tunnel of fire.

As the date for my World Record attempt drew closer, I began taping with NBC and setting up my new motorcycle. My girlfriend at the time was very supportive and excited for me, and she even took part in some of the filming for the show. My parents were asked to give an interview on camera about the record attempt, and they became more concerned and nervous for me as the event drew closer. By the beginning of January, I was seeing commercials for the event on TV and I began to get calls for radio, magazine, and personal appearances. The offers were lining up "if" I could successfully pull this stunt off.

The day before the record attempt, I got up early and was at Universal before filming started. I took it upon myself to walk around the lot so that I could relax a bit and enjoy the experience—and when I say walk around the lot, I mean "ride my stunt bike without permission around Universal Studios." I went by the famous great white shark attraction, then over to the Clock Tower from Back to the Future. It was a chance for me to clear my head and focus on the task at hand.

I wanted a chance to walk the tunnel by myself so that I could get a feeling of the space and length and magnitude of what I was about to attempt. I felt like I was a caged animal while walking the tunnel.

There was metal tubing completely surrounding me, and the thought of flames pointed directly at me during this 200-foot ride was getting me nervous, to say the least. I remember walking the tunnel and thinking that it seemed longer than 200 feet.

As this was a live show, they wanted to get a real reaction from lighting up the tunnel for the first time, and since it was a 200-foot tunnel of fire it was guaranteed to be a spectacle. This tunnel was a custom-built, 200-foot, fire-breathing machine. It was constructed with metal tubing and hooked up with two semi trucks pumping propane gas through pipes with what must have been 2,000 holes pointed down into the tunnel. Production began clearing the set, and the cameras began to roll as ignition of the tunnel for the first time was about to commence.

In 5... 4... 3... 2... 1.... and ignition, as the tunnel lit up for the first time. I could feel the heat a couple hundred feet away and hear the high-pitched sound of the gas being fed through the pipes. This was definitely a sight to see, and in my case a sight to ride through.

My initial reaction was, holy shit! I'm supposed to ride my motorcycle 200 feet through this inferno? It was so hot, the camera and sound crew had to back up from where they had previously been staged for shooting. The tunnel had only been lit for 2 minutes, and already there were growing concerns that it might be putting off so much heat it would ignite nearby buildings. The heat was so intense; it was popping the pavement along the bottom of the tunnel. Things had just gotten real!

The time had come to start suiting up, which meant putting on the first layer of fire-retardant suit and being dipped in fire-retardant jelly.

The irony of the situation was that it was freezing putting on the first suit filled with cold jelly. The outer layer was a dry fire-retardant, and it was my first barrier against the flames. Walking outside and getting over to my bike, I watched as they prepped for lighting the tunnel a second time. It was about 6:00 in the evening, and to this day I will never forget watching the tunnel light up against the dark sky. The propone flowing through the pipes whistled louder than ever, and the heat was so intense I could feel it from my trailer 50 yards away. I began to notice one of the firemen pointing a thermostat gun at the tunnel. He was measuring the heat coming off the tunnel, and as he looked over at me I could read the look of concern in his face. He said, "Clint, we thought the tunnel would be close to 1200°F, but as it turns out, it's 2000°F!"

As I fired up the bike to "warm" her up, I was stationed 150 feet in front of the tunnel, staring directly down into the belly of the fire. I couldn't keep my eyes off her. I'm not sure if that was my concentration being at its peak or simply the fact that I had never seen such a magnificent display of fire in my life. Now it was time for my helmet. A helmet may seem like just another piece of equipment to most people, but for me, when my helmet goes on, I feel as though I transform. I immediately feel a rush of energy and composure all at once. This may seem silly, but since the age of 8, I had been putting on a helmet. It was always the last piece of equipment to go on before I rode. It became a flip of the switch, so to speak, changing me from the normal, everyday, happy-go-lucky Clint Ewing to the Clint Ewing that performs.

Looking at the tunnel, I couldn't see in more than 10 feet. I knew I would just have to trust my instincts and do the best I could 10 feet at a time, as fast as I could. It was a strange thing, to be sitting on a motorcycle in the middle of Universal Studios, next to studio sets from my favorite movies and TV shows as a kid. I received the signal that filming had commenced and that I was to go after a 10 second countdown.

5... 4... 3... 2... 1... I let out the clutch and twisted the throttle in heavy acceleration. If the motorcycle shut off in the tunnel from lack of oxygen, the very least I could do was get as much speed as possible to try and make the distance.

The closer I got to the tunnel, the hotter it became. I could feel the heat building as I got closer and closer to the entrance. As I entered the tunnel I was taken aback by the spectacle of light and the heat being blown into me, while the whistling of the propane being fed through the pipes was even more pronounced within the tunnel.

I knew I must remember not to breathe, as the heat would immediately enter my lungs and burn me from the inside out. I remember thinking for the first half of the tunnel that the heat wasn't so bad, but by the halfway point, that feeling had changed. Even with the layers of protection I was feeling the 2000 degrees on my back—literally.

As I got closer to what should have been the end of the tunnel, I was fighting to see the exit, with fire raining down on me and bouncing off the front lens of my helmet. It began to feel like my back was on fire, but the only thing I wanted to focus on was getting to the exit.

Just as I started to think I would never see the end of the tunnel, I began to recognize a dark spot in the middle of my vision. This dark spot turned out to be the end of the tunnel and the only spot in my vision not filled with fire. This was my exit point! As I exited the tunnel I felt a rush of fresh air and cool sensation on the front of my body, but my backside was still feeling the heat.

I tossed the bike down and got down to the ground as quickly as possible. I was still holding my breath, and it was a good thing I was, because just then I was doused with a shower of fire extinguishers by the fireman on set. A cloud of white powder filled the air. When I finally couldn't hold my breath any longer, I took a deep gasp for air that couldn't have felt any sweeter. Jumping up to inspect my suit, I realized that my back really had been on fire during the tunnel ride and that it wasn't just my imagination running wild during the ride.

Even the bottom of my motorcycle had caught fire. As I took off the helmet, the cameras were in my face and ready for the interview.

They wanted to know what it felt like and what emotions were going through my mind.

The first thing that popped into my head was, that was one hell of a ride!

I barely made it through from a lack of vision and 2000 degrees literally riding my back. After the interview, it was brought to my attention that my family was leaving. Production had informed my parents before consulting me that they would be asking me to attempt the record a second time, for live recording reasons.

This infuriated my parents, because I was now being asked to attempt this dangerous stunt twice. Of course I would prefer not to tempt the devil again, but I was warned about breaking my contract if I didn't make multiple attempts.

As my parents were leaving that night to head home, I hugged them and told them I understood their decision to leave. They informed me that they couldn't be a part of something where my safety wasn't in the production's best interest.

My father said, "You don't have to prove anything to anyone."

My reply was simple:

"I only have to prove to myself I can do this."

My father knew me well enough to know I wouldn't back down from this, and he left without argument. I was happy they at least had the chance to watch me the first time and was there for support.

I cleaned up in the shower at the Universal lot, and kept thinking to myself how happy I was that this stunt was halfway over.

That night I went back to my hotel thinking about one thing only. I was focused on the tunnel and how I could make sure I made it through again, this time on live TV. I knew from the reactions of my family, friends, and managers that this tunnel scared pretty much everyone there. Like the jumps when I rode dirt bikes, this was just another hurdle for me to accomplish. I got to bed early that night, anxious to get up and defeat this tunnel.

Since my family had left the day before, Production had asked more of my friends to come onto set in order to fill the void. They also rallied the "support" of a few celebrities from current NBC shows. It wasn't my family, but it sure was funny to look over and see celebrities cheering for me that I had never met. Sure, my parents had decided not to stay and that stung a bit, but the fact remained that I was going for this record alone—and alone, it would be.

The stunt was almost a mirror image of the night before. At 6pm I was geared up, sitting on the bike, and ready for the countdown. This time it was LIVE, so everyone was on point and there to do business. I sat there thinking about what had worked for me the night before. I was calm and collected, with no distractions, and only one gasp of breath away from accomplishing what I had set out to do.

In 5… 4… 3… 2… 1…Here we go again, and this time I relied on my experience from the night before.

I had to gain as much speed as possible in case the bike ran out of air and try to find the dark spot in the middle of tunnel as my exit point. I attempted to crouch down closer to the bike so the fire bouncing off me wouldn't have such an easy target this time around. At the halfway point, again I was feeling the heat but I was steadfast in looking for my outlet. It was there within seconds, and I was still holding my breath. At the exit my back was very hot, and I wouldn't take the chance of it catching on fire again, so as I exited the tunnel I tossed the bike down. This time around I didn't catch on fire, and neither did the bike.

I jumped up to the set of cameras to be interviewed about my experience and the fact that I had officially broken the Guinness World Record for longest motorcycle ride through a tunnel of fire. Guinness was there in person to award the certificate and congratulate me. It felt amazing to be called a Guinness World Record holder, though to be honest, the best feeling of all was the fact that I didn't have to do it again.

The magnitude of what had just transpired really hadn't hit me yet. There had been so much filming, training, and work that had gone into the stunt, and within two days it was all over. It was sad to look over and not see my parents and brother cheering me on, but I knew they would be proud. I was done filming, so I headed back to my hotel in Hollywood. My friends were with me, along with my then girlfriend. By the time I had showered and come back down in the lobby, the "live" show was already being played on national TV. My friends began to celebrate, as they knew how the story would end. Hotel management began to get upset, as my friends were drinking and getting louder with excitement as the finale of the show got closer. As the interview portion of the show and the awarding of the certificate began, my longtime friend began to yell with excitement. Yes, he was there for it live, but he was even more excited watching it on TV—or perhaps it was the liquor adding to the excitement. This time, management came over and asked him to keep it down. My friend's response: "That's my friend Clint Ewing, breaking a Guinness World Record on NBC. When will this ever happen again?!"

Little did either of us know that I would be attempting to regain this record just five years later.

4 GRASS IS ALWAYS GREENER

I will never forget the day I made the decision to focus my attention on riding full time as a professional sportbike freestyler rider. Since that day, there have been some amazing and some not-so-amazing times. With the highs, there are also the lows. You just do your best to make sure there are more positive times than negative.

For any professional athlete, practice is very important, and for me practice meant three times a week, pushing myself to learn new tricks and trying to perform them live to the best of my ability. Through the years, I learned that there are certain tricks that are a must for every rider. One of them is performing a stoppie.

Riding the front wheel and balancing this for as long as you can set you apart from other riders and is a direct correlation to how good you are as a rider. The downfall of this trick is that, no matter how good you are, sooner or later you will crash — and when you do, it normally goes very badly. As you can imagine, accelerating a motorcycle then quickly applying just enough brake but not too much, in order to not go over the handlebars, takes a certain level of finesse.

The longer the distance you want to go, the more practice it takes and the riskier it will be. Longer distances require greater speed and thus a higher level of danger. I was average at this trick and wished to push myself to the next level. I was typically rolling 200 feet at around 50 mph, but I felt it was time to step up my game a bit and reach the 300-foot mark.

After practicing for weeks, I was up to around 70 mph and

averaging 300 feet. I had reached my goal, but I had to also ensure that I would be consistent during shows — or as I call it, "on lock."

During my performances, I always want to perform the most up-to-date tricks I know and put on the best show that I can. It was a Thursday evening at the practice spot, and I was with a friend. I was feeling good and had been balancing the bike well that night and closing in on reaching 350 feet.

I snapped the throttle and began my approach like I had done hundreds of other times that week, this time set on breaking the 350-foot mark. At 70 mph I backed off the throttle, and I let one second too long go by before I applied the front brake. This lull in braking created a bounce within the front suspension that was ever so slight, but enough for my front end to slide out from underneath me as the rear end of the bike came up over my head.

This all happened so quickly that, within a split moment, I found myself sliding across the pavement face first with the bike on top of me. It felt like slow motion as my face was pressed against the pavement, and all I could see was the surface passing by inches from my face. My motorcycle had literally body slammed me into the pavement at 70 mph before dragging me to a stop.

My buddy ran over to ask if I was okay. Okay? Sure! I just got tossed down the road by my own motorcycle; I was doing great! I couldn't even reply, though, as the wind had been knocked out of me — and as anyone that has had this happen will know, it felt awful. My friend continued to ask if I was okay, but I couldn't catch my breath to answer.

My breath had been involuntarily pounded out of my lungs. As I got up, I could tell that something was wrong with my shoulder, and it was a feeling I have had before as well. My shoulder had been pushed out of its socket, and I knew I could either talk about it or get it back into place before it started to swell up and become worse.

1… 2….3! I pushed the bottom of my elbow straight up into the air, and I could feel my shoulder pop back into the socket. My friend packed up the bike, and I headed to the hospital. I knew something else was wrong with my back, but I wouldn't know what until I could have someone take a look at it. The doctor gave me a look over and it felt like that was all it was, a quick glance. I told him I was feeling chest pain and back pain and was told it was due to inflammation, but I wasn't so sure. I have had swelling before from accidents, but this was different, and I told him I thought something was busted. He got me a sling for my dislocated shoulder and told me I should go home and get some rest. After I got home, my girlfriend came by to check on me and offer some help if needed.

That night, I couldn't sleep and my back continued to throb. The next day I went back into the hospital for an X-ray, because I still felt like something more than inflammation was going on. This time, the doctor came back with news that my right shoulder blade had a lateral fracture and that I would be off the bike for months. I was definitely not having a good week, since I knew that meant I would have to cancel a large show I was scheduled to perform at later that month. That evening, I got back home and realized my girlfriend had left her laptop at my place.

When I tried to get in touch with her, she didn't answer. She had been acting strangely for the last few weeks, and I started to get the feeling that something was up.

Normally I am a very trusting person, but when I opened up her laptop and discovered her home screen had a picture of another guy on it, I felt as though my trust had been misplaced. When she called back I calmly notified her of my findings and said that we would no longer be dating. Two years of dating, and now I was left handicapped and alone.

It's a good thing I can tolerate a lot, as I was getting hit from all sides! Later that evening my friends came over to cheer me up and take my mind off things. For the next few weeks, I slowly began to get my motorcycle back up to running condition while giving my body a rest. Both had been through a lot, but the motorcycle was far easier to fix than myself.

One night my ex called me late at night and told me she was having issues with her new boyfriend, and she asked if I would drive downtown to pick her up and take her away. I remember thinking, this woman has the audacity to call me after she cheated on me to ask for my help? She must really need my help! So I did what any self-respecting man would do; I reminded her that she had gotten rid of an honest and loyal boyfriend in exchange for what she had now… then I hung up.

Since I now had plenty of time on my hands, I set my sites on lining up a show at a motorcycle track where I had always wanted to perform: Laguna Seca Raceway, a world-renowned track located in

Monterey, California. Known for its beauty and layout in a natural hill setting, this was a track I had always wanted to ride. Motorcycle, car, and even bicycle races had been held at this track for over 50 years.

I set myself a goal that I would come back from this accident and perform for one of the most prestigious raceways in the United States. After doing a little research, I found the name of the Track Coordinator, and I sent her a general email about whether I could possibly perform at the venue during the upcoming superbike race.

When there was no reply, I tried to think of a different method to catch her attention. Every woman loves flowers, right? Twenty minutes later I was on the phone, ordering up a dozen roses to Laguna Seca, with a personalized card that read,

"I wheelie want to perform for you."

The next day I received a call from her, and I was told my method of getting her attention was unique and justified an answer. I gave her my little spiel—and two months later, I found myself driving up to Laguna Seca to perform for the AMA superbike races. Knowing this was a big event for me, with an estimated 30,000 spectators to perform in front of, I was taking this event very seriously. My bike was back together, and I had been able to practice for a few weeks since coming off my injury.

I was not at 100%, but I was hungry to perform and excited to do it at such a venue. For this large-scale event I hired two models I had never worked with but who had extensive promotional experience, which was what I was looking for. Arriving in Monterey on Friday afternoon, I met with track officials and went over the logistics of the performance as well as the location of my booth during the races. That evening I met up with the models and went over what I required from them. Later that evening, my friend Phil came by to pick up tickets for himself and a friend.

The next morning, I got up at 6 am and headed to the track so I could set up early and be ready for spectators to come by the booth. I had a great spot in the fairway and knew this location would get a lot of traffic.

As the models arrived, one of the girls told me her friend wanted to join and help out as well. So I had the three of them set up the booth while I prepped my bike for the show at noon. Soon spectators started coming in and asking for posters, hats, shirts, and pictures. It felt good to be performing again for the first time since my nasty spill.

Our booth was busier than ever, and it certainly didn't hurt that I was on the flyer for the weekend and had three beautiful ladies at the booth. Track officials notified me I had 30 minutes until show time. I walked the bike over to the staging area, with one of the promotional models holding a Dunlop umbrella and walking in high heels.

Spectators were most likely checking out the girl, but in less than 15 minutes I would have all eyes on me. I had a little practice area on the side of the track where I was getting warmed up.

Two minutes left until go time, and my heart was beating with anticipation. I had no worries in the world and began to visualize my routine. Since this track was so large, my performance wouldn't be the normal 20 minutes. I would perform at the front straight away for 15 minutes, then at a second and third location for another 15 minutes each.

The whole performance would run for 45 minutes, so I had to make sure I paced myself. As the final lap of the race came to end, the pace car came up beside me and instructed me to follow him to my first performance location.

As I was given the green flag to head around the corner to the front straight away, a quick thought entered my mind: Have fun. I shot down the straight away in a nice long wheelie to start off the performance, with thousands of spectators to my right and left. I was feeling good and going through my performance with grace and ease.

I was landing all the tricks I had practiced and began to fall into a groove. As I looked over at the pace car I noticed a checkered flag waving outside the window, which meant I was to follow it to the second performance area of the track. As I accelerated heavily over the hill and into turn 1, I tried to calm my nerves and take some deeps breaths, as I wasn't even halfway done yet.

The second spot was between turns 3 and 4 and had been specially selected, due to my sponsor Dunlop Tires' large banner over that section of the raceway. Now, for most, this may not seem like anything, but for me it gave me a sense of pride for the company I represent and the honor of riding for them. I wanted to do my best, and I was giving it everything I had. I was throwing every trick I knew into my performance, but I was also losing energy. My arms began to tighten up and the bike began to get hot due to the length of the performance and the temperature on the track. The brake pads began to fade a bit from excessive use and heat.

But I was saved by the flag, as the pace car waved me onto the third and final performance area. As the pace car accelerated quickly up the hill to the back part of Laguna Seca, I could see the bridge that hung over the raceway after turn 5.

There were a bunch of spectators looking down over the raceway, and I began to think how cool it would be to wheelie up the hill, with them looking down at me while I passed by underneath. At the bottom of the hill, I dumped the clutch and brought the front wheel up. I was standing on the back seat in a wheelie and had a sudden feeling that came over me quickly. I felt as though I was on top of the world and I was completely locked into this moment. I thought that, through the hardships, there were also positive outcomes, and this was one of them. I was happy and excited at the same time, and I began to nod my head up and down as if I were saying yes repeatedly to myself.

As I raced under the bridge, I remember thinking what an amazing experience this was and that I should cherish this moment. I had gone down in a violent crash months ago, and now I found myself performing at Laguna Raceway in front of thousands of spectators.

This moment was mine.

As I made my way to the last performance area on the track, I noticed one thing. I was being asked to perform in the most famous part of the track, but also the most difficult.

The pace car stopped at the foot of the Corkscrew. It was a corner in the track with a 50-foot drop.

During the races, this was a great place to watch the riders speed down the hill and position themselves to pass each other, but for me it was something completely new.

I had never performed stunts on such a steep hill. I looked over to the pace car and accelerated down the hill. I wanted to see what I could do on this portion of the track and still do my best to entertain. From the bottom of the hill looking up, it looked like every bit of a 50 foot incline, and as I began my ascent up the hill, I popped the clutch and brought the front wheel up for a wheelie.

Now, positioning oneself in a wheelie is one thing, but positioning while going up a three-story incline turn was another. Halfway up the hill, I began to lean more forward as I could feel gravity pulling me backwards.

As I made it up the hill, the spectators cheered with excitement. This motivated me to try to wheelie back down the hill. But as I brought the front wheel up at the top of the Corkscrew I began to feel a heavy pull on my front wheel, and I knew the best thing to do was to bring it down before I fell off the bike and watched my motorcycle ghost ride itself down the rest of the hill. After a couple of burnouts and some wheelies at the top, I decided I had better bring this show to a close, as I was tired from performing and riding around the track for what seemed like forever.

Coming into the pits, I received praise from spectators, and I saw that my booth had a nice-sized line at it for autographs.

As I got off my bike, I noticed that SpeedTV immediately started filming my promo girls and the spectators. An hour later I had completed signing and I was exhausted. Performing is a lot of the fun I get from riding, but I also enjoy seeing people who are genuinely happy.

The best part is seeing a kid's reaction to a free poster, hat, or a picture on the motorcycle. It brings back my younger days, when I was a kid at a professional baseball game, waiting in line for a player to sign my hat. That memory reminds me how important it is to take the time for the fans and especially kids at the shows. It may only be a second of my life, but for a child the impression on them could last a lifetime.

By the end of race day we had successfully handed out all the hats, stickers, and posters and were looking forward to a nice hot meal and some drinks down in the well-known street in Monterey known as Cannery Row.

Cannery Row during a normal tourist visit is beautiful, with beach-front restaurants and bars, but during a race weekend it becomes party central. After getting back to the hotel and cleaning up, I headed out for the evening with three of the models and a few of my friends.

Cannery Row was lined with hundreds of motorcycles and the

bars and restaurants were packed. We decided to hit as many bars as we could that night, and this town was full of them. After the first few bars, it was more than obvious that our drinking pace was picking up. At the third bar I ran into a photographer from Super StreetBike Magazine who had seen my performance and wanted to get a picture of me downtown.

I decided it would probably be best to include the whole bunch of us in the shot, and to this day that photo is one of my favorites. We stood in the middle of Cannery Row with models and all. My really good friend Chris, who's not into bikes, was so disinterested the photo caught him knuckle deep in a dessert he was eating.

For the rest of us, it was an amazing night filled with the coolest bikes, drinks, food, and entertainment.

For our last stop of the night we decided to stop at a British pub, The Crown Anchor.

By now I was slamming down water because I had another day of riding ahead of me, but the rest of the crew were living it up. I saw countless guys hitting on the promo girls, drinks being bought, and friends dancing and singing.

It felt great to be back doing what I do, but it also felt great to bring my friends together.

Throughout the years I have noticed that some of my friends' girlfriends don't especially like me. It took me some time to understand, but I finally realized that my friends' girls don't like it when I come by because I'm unpredictable. I bring beautiful girls with me, go out for drinks, and usually have a bit of fun. I have learned that what I do is break up the norm for some people. I shake things up and bring a sense of uncertainty into a situation or evening. As I sat there and looked upon the group, I began to reflect on all the good times I have had and to remember that situations are what you make of them.

For me, almost any situation is an opportunity to make an amazing memory.

Months ago I was laid up in bed and had been cheated on by my ex; now, I had fulfilled a dream of performing at Laguna Seca and was able to share that moment with friends. Sometimes I feel I am at my best when I'm either down on my luck or I'm told I can't do something. Lucky for me, there would be plenty more of this in my future!

5 CREATE THE NOW

Riding a motorcycle for a living is as fun as it sounds. There are the occasional downfalls like broken bones, but there is also one thing in particular that makes what I do so much fun…creativity.

I can be creative in the way I ride, take pictures, make videos, and ultimately live my life.

When I was a kid, I would sit with my brother and watch episodes of CHiPs, an early 1980s TV show about two California highway patrol officers who rode the highways of Los Angeles on their Kawasaki motorcycles. I was one of the kids that never wanted to be a cop, but I wanted to be able to ride a motorcycle everywhere and do as I pleased.

That was at least the idea in my head of what cops did when I was five, but as I got older, I figured out that highway patrol had to actually cite people for traffic violations. I do most of my heavy thinking at night when I have settled down and had a chance to catch up with the day. One evening when I was lying in bed, I got an idea that made me literally pop up. I had to get this idea written out before I could fall asleep. I quickly jotted down the idea to be the ultimate cop. I would go back in time to 1980 and film my version of how CHiPs would have played out if I was a lead character.

Early the next day I began looking around for an old CHP motorcycle. I also called my videographer and filled him in on my idea. For the most part whenever I come up with an idea and people hear about it, they say one of two things: "No way you're going to do

3

it" or "That's just crazy." If I hear one of these reactions, it's usually a good sign that I should do it because that means it's a new idea or so farfetched that nobody has done it.

So the plan began to unfold, and all I had to do was get a retired police motorcycle and police outfit, chase a girl around town on her motorcycle, video everything, and not get caught doing it.

Obviously I can't go down to the local police station and purchase a motorcycle from them, so I purchased a used retired police motorcycle and started equipping it with a siren, red and blue lights, and a set of CHP decals for the tank.

The police outfit was a bit easier as I had an old friend who I talked into lending me his uniform. I called up a sponsor and had them send me a blank old-school helmet I could outfit with CHP logos and then topped it off with a set of boots and 1980s-style sunglasses. I didn't want to chase just anyone across town; I wanted it to be a beautiful woman who could also ride well.

Took me a few weeks, but I found the perfect woman for it.

She was a short brunette, large busted, and had years of riding experience under her belt.

Lastly, it was time to set up how and where we would film this.

The plan was to shoot over a two-day period while trying not to get arrested for impersonating a police officer.

We started shooting at 7am, and for the first part of the shoot we wanted to depict a lazy officer eating donuts with one hand and with the other holding a radar gun.

Not 20 minutes went by, and we soon figured out that this might be harder than originally planned. Traffic was slowing down, looking to see what was going on, and we had to shoot a few times in order to get the shots we wanted.

We were starting to attract a lot of attention, and we weren't even done with the first shot of the video.

Chasing her down some side streets seemed a bit easier as we kept moving, and the videographer could film as he drove next to us. As we arrived at the second location, I knew this would be a challenge. My idea on paper was to have the female rider lose me on the side streets and make her way into a car wash where she would be hiding.

We needed time to set this up, and it was busy with cars. I parked the "police bike" in one of the stalls and blocked it off so we could use it. I started to feel the power of the uniform and that got me nervous.

We shot a half dozen takes of me looking for her, her spraying me in the face with water, and a few of me drifting the motorcycle while chasing after her out of the car wash.

As you can imagine, this got a lot of attention, and we started feeling the pressure to get out of there before we got into trouble.

Just as we were packing up, one of the ladies in the lot said she called the cops. I told everyone to meet at a burger joint, and all three of us split up.

As I crossed through an intersection, I saw two police cars racing to the car wash, sirens blaring. Meeting up at the burger joint, we decided it would be best to get some footage away from this location, so we headed out to the beach to set up our next scene. We needed some freeway footage, so I made my way to the freeway, and as I approached the onramp, I began to accelerate to make for some high speed shots.

As I looked over to the side of me, there was a highway patrol car already on the freeway, and I thought, this is it, I am definitely going to jail now! Act casual, Clint, don't look over, and act cool. Act the part, Clint, and maybe they won't notice your police motorcycle is outdated and that your uniform is not CHP-issued. If they do notice, you are definitely going to jail, and I couldn't imagine having to call up my family or friends and explain to them why I had been arrested.

What seemed like forever but was actually a few seconds went by, and I casually nodded as the CHP began to pass me. The next exit wasn't for another mile, and all I could do was stay in my lane and play the part of a true officer of the law. I got off at the next exit and made a few zig zags in business park and took a break behind another building.

We met up and discussed the repercussions of being caught filming this. Each of us would be in trouble if caught.

Everyone was in after deciding I would take the rap for it. This was my idea and a video for me, so I wouldn't let everyone go down with the ship. Next location would be a bit more private since it was my practice spot.

The motorcycle was feeling a bit funny after doing some wheelies and drifts. This bike was nearly 500 lbs and wasn't built for stunts. After filming some stuff in the dirt and jumping a curb I could feel the integrity of the bike breaking down. It was becoming harder to start, and the front forks blew oil out all over the ground.

The wheelies had proven to be too much for this bike. As a kid I had always wondered what it would be like to be a cop, and today I was as close as I was going to get.

Chasing this woman across town doing burnouts, drifts, wheelies, and riding through the dirt was as much fun as it sounds. Having the real cops on my heels was merely an added bonus of adrenaline rush. I wanted to end this film in style and thought what better way than to literally run her down and bust her like you see on TV.

With my videographer filming up close, I cornered her in a parking lot and began the chase on foot. I jumped off the motorcycle and tackled her while she ran. After a few takes the bike had a flat tire and bent rim, and I also gave the girl a charley horse from landing on her leg.

It became more than apparent that this bike wouldn't withstand a second day of filming. We had shot for nearly seven hours, and the bike would barely start. For our last location I needed somewhere private with a cool backdrop and needed a shot of the girl coming towards the camera with me chasing behind in a wheelie. After the second take I noticed a cop ride by on a motorcycle and look over. Oh crap!

I quickly rode up to my video guy and asked him if there was a cop riding up behind me; the answer was yes. This was it, I was definitely in trouble now, and there was no way of getting out of this one.

Within seconds the CHP motorcycle came up beside me, and the look on his face was priceless. He sat there for what seemed like a minute with a look of disbelief and wonder. Literally after 10 seconds or so he says,

"What the hell is this?"

Now I had not counted on coming up with an excuse to use if caught by the police, but I quickly came up with one. I am a professional sportbike freestyle rider, and one of my friends works for the Police Department. I am making a short video poking fun at him.

There seemed to be yet another pause of silence. He was either thinking that this was a load of crap or that nobody in their right mind could make this up.

He broke his silence with a quick but stern statement:

"As long as you stay on private property and do not set foot on public road, I have no problem with what you are doing."

That could have gone bad, but instead I was free to finish the rest of the scene. It was probably the fact that he didn't want to deal with us that helped us out of that situation. Minutes later I was filming a nice wheelie, and the motorcycle lost power almost instantly. The front wheel came down hard, and I heard a loud explosion from the front tire popping. This bike was done, and so was our filming.

The video was made for YouTube and did ok but never seemed to take off in the way I intended. Years later I was able to use it on Instagram, and it seemed to do much better there.

Sometimes things don't go as intended, but as long as you're trying and putting forth effort, it sure beats sitting at home.

6 DANCE WITH THE DEVIL

It's 2013, and I am staring down a 365-foot tunnel of fire at the largest motorcycle rally in the United States in Sturgis, South Dakota.

How did I get to this point?

It had been five years since I set the Guinness world record at Universal Studios. Since it was televised on national TV, it received a lot of recognition, which brought attempts to defeat my record.

Since 2008, there had been a few attempts to break my record with one being fatal and another successful. The record was broken by two South Africans riding a sidecar with three wheels, which is considered a motorcycle.

With this Guinness attempt gaining in popularity, there was more interest in bringing it back to the States.

I received a call from CMT television that they were interested in having me perform this longer tunnel of fire during the largest motorcycle rally in the Unites States, the Sturgis Rally in South Dakota. Sturgis is a week-long motorcycle rally with everything from visiting Mount Rushmore, rock 'n' roll concerts, parties, tattoos and for this year, a world record attempt.

Attendance for 2013 was over 470,000 people within a town of normally 6,800. The locals either stay in town to make money or take off for vacation to get away from the storm of riders coming through. Some locals will rent out their house so riders can eat, sleep, and park. This, in return, pays for their vacation once a year!

I have been performing at the Buffalo Chip Campground since 2009, and it has always been a lot of fun. It's the only place I have ever performed at where, while I am riding, there are also girls dancing on stripper poles and well-known performing artists like Ozzy Osbourne, ZZ top, Kid Rock, etc. playing in the background LIVE.

I remember that my first year there was a clash of the titans, so to speak. An estimated 90% of the riders at Sturgis ride Harleys, so when I came into town for the first year I showed up with my two Japanese bikes. I performed for the week doing stunts throughout the day and received a lot of attention, some positive but also some negative. I was literally one of a handful of riders in the whole town not riding a Harley and could feel the negative thoughts circulate among some spectators before every performance. The more I rode and the harder I performed the more respect I would earn.

Over the years my performances received more and more attention, and by 2013 I was being asked to regain my Guinness world record at one of the largest motorcycle venues in the United States.

Filming had started in California with CMT television and like the first world record attempt, they began filming the back story of who Clint Ewing was.

Needless to say, my family wasn't very happy to hear that I would be trying to regain the world record. After filming for a couple of weeks with filler content, it was time to make the two-day drive out to South Dakota.

This year I would be driving out with a few friends and my girlfriend at the time. The first stop from California was Nevada to pick up my buddy Troy. It was nice to kick start the trip with a night out in Vegas. Knowing I had an important record to attempt, I told myself and others I wouldn't be drinking or partying. I wanted to stay focused and in shape for the task at hand. After Vegas our next stop was Salt Lake City, Utah, which was spent having a second night out drinking and having fun.

Normally this trip was done in 24 hours, but this year I had people along for the ride, and I couldn't do my normal iron butt drive with minimal stops. Finally, by the third day we had arrived at the Buffalo Chip Campground in Sturgis, South Dakota.

The scene at the Buffalo Chip is amazing with 600 acres filled with RVs, motorcycles, and the concert hall. It's definitely a sight to see, and during concerts at night it's electrifying with thousands of bikers. The saving grace that kept me from getting sucked into the night life was to have my performances during the day and rest at night in the RV. This allowed a home base during the week to relax and get rest without the daily craziness.

I love having fun as much as, if not more, than the next guy, but drinking beers and throwing midgets down a life-size outdoor bowling alley doesn't prepare me for setting a world record.

Now this didn't stop the rest of my friends from having fun that week, but I was there to set a record, and every day after my stunt shows I would go back to the RV to eat and rest. Thursday, better known as Tunnel of Fire Day, had finally arrived.

I took an early morning ride on a motorcycle up to Mount Rushmore to show my girlfriend and friends the beautiful sight. It allowed me to relax that morning and concentrate on what was to come later that evening. It felt amazing to share the experience of riding through the black hills of South Dakota with my girlfriend and friends.

So much history in that area, and it was alive with hundreds of thousands of riders. We pulled off to the side of the road to snap a photo of the group in front of Mount Rushmore. Upon riding back to the Buffalo Chip, I had seven radio spots to interview with before I began getting myself ready for the tunnel.

I literally ran from each radio station to the next talking about what got me into riding and what I was feeling while getting ready for this attempt.

After my interviews I headed back to the RV to get my bike and myself ready to film and set another record. Leading up to this day, my friends were confident in me and believed I could do what I set out to do. The excitement turned into a quiet tone of concern that day as my friends had a chance to walk the 365 feet with me. The 365 feet didn't sound that long, but from my previous experience with my first world record, I knew it would be a long time to navigate while on fire.

During the walk to the end of the tunnel, I could see the concern in their faces. It was the length of a football field filled with darkness, although each of them was imagining the ride while on fire. As I began suiting up and filming for the show, I tuned everything out except for the tunnel.

I focused on settling my nerves and not thinking about anything other than riding through the tunnel and succeeding. Suiting up next to my friends and girlfriend, I knew the seriousness of the stunt I was about to perform.

It was just five years previously that I had the same feeling in my stomach: confidence. Before I jumped on my bike and headed to the staging area, my friends gathered around to wish me luck. Minutes later I was staged 300 feet away, facing the entrance of the tunnel. As before all performances, especially ones of this magnitude, I found myself in a zone.

I hate to call it that, but it seems to really fit what happens to me after I put on my helmet. I have no worries in the world, and once the helmet comes down, I have a different outlook on what I am capable of.

My friends describe it as a second personality, but to me it's the absence of a personality.

When the helmet goes on, it signifies business!

The plan was set out for me and everyone coordinating on the stunt from the fire crew, film crew, stunt crew, and Guinness. Once the fire was set, I was to give it a few seconds to burn evenly then go as I saw fit. The tunnel was set up differently than the previous record but was up to the standards.

The fire was to be set using 20 or so people on each side of the tunnel to light the torches then light the tunnel. The countdown from 10 had begun, and as the tunnel started to ignite, I could see it rapidly spreading throughout the length of the tunnel. I could see a small window of opportunity to make it the 365 feet to the end. Within 15 seconds of lighting the tunnel, I could see people running back from the heat. It was a spectacle of 365 feet of tunnel burning against the South Dakota sky.

As I was about to take off, I received notification not to go.

I had no idea what was going on, but my adrenaline was at an all-time high.

What seemed like an eternity of waiting turned out to really be about 20 seconds, but that ended up costing me more than I could give up.

My window of opportunity was getting smaller by the second. Getting the all clear, I clutched the bike and quickly accelerated to the tunnel.

What was once a feasible stunt quickly turned into the near impossible from just a 20-second delay.

As I got closer and closer to the entrance, I could see "my tunnel" become an inferno rather than an even burn.

I have been asked many times why I even went for it after the delay. It's just who I am. I don't look for reasons to give up. I look for ways to achieve.

As I made my first 10 feet into the tunnel, I was carrying a bit of speed, as I knew my window of opportunity to make it the 365 feet was quickly diminishing, if not closed.

By the 100-foot mark I knew I was in big trouble. My vision had become drastically impaired with a storm of fire bouncing off my helmet along with my motorcycle beginning to lose power. I made the choice to stick it out as I remember thinking that this could pass within moments, but as I encountered the next 50 or so feet, the situation had not changed. Fire continually bounced off my visor, and the bike nearly stopped running.

I had practiced that if the bike were to turn off I would pull in the clutch and coast as much as I could. I didn't think I would actually be doing it. I was, and I must have coasted another 100+ feet or so before my equilibrium was thrown off. It was similar to being drunk and then lying down, and the room starts spinning out of control.

The only difference was that my eyes were wide open, and I was riding a motorcycle at 55mph with fire bouncing off my hands and face.

The fire blocked all my vision and started pulling back the first of two lenses that covered my face. There was a thought in my head for a moment that I was definitely ghost riding this motorcycle right then. I made the decision that if I was to go on any longer this might be the end. I went with my instincts while still holding my breath and chose to veer left to exit the tunnel.

With the bike completely not running and no vision, I slammed down hard against the ground and slid into a steel pole holding up the tunnel. I had never been so happy to hit a pole in my life!

This instantly gave me a reference point as to where I was in this inferno. Jumping to my left, I had made the right choice and had broken through the flames. I took the biggest breath of fresh air, although I knew something was wrong instantly as my hands felt as though they were on fire.

Oh wait, they were!

I instinctually shook my hands to notice my gloves had flown off along with the skin. My hands literally melted off, and I was not 10 feet from the fire fighter before he began to douse my hands with water. My dance with the devil had nearly taken my life, but not this time.

From the shock of what just transpired, the pain had not set in yet. One of the first guys on the scene was my buddy Jon who, along with the fire fighter, got me up on my feet. As I stood feet from the tunnel, I could see my bike burning in front of me.

A sudden disappointment shrouded my entire body, and I began to feel like I had let my friends, family, and sponsors down. As I sat down in the ambulance, the pain quickly set in. I looked down at my hands and saw my skin had literally been burned away. My back was also very warm, but compared to my hands, I couldn't see the damage. Two bags of morphine later, I was still in a great amount of pain.

With years of broken bones and injuries I tried to remain calm and composed.

After 20 minutes at the local hospital, my friends and I started getting a bad feeling about my care. The local doctor, while attending to my wounds, was telling me that I would be ok after a few weeks of recovery. Even with a few bags of morphine in me, I knew this was either a lie or stupidity. I knew I had to get out of that hospital ASAP.

My friends and girlfriend knew the damage was far worse, and for some reason this doctor was not correct with her diagnoses. My friends made the decision that we would leave immediately after I had been bandaged up. We made our way back to the Buffalo Chip, and after arriving, the producer of the show asked if I would be willing to sit down for a few minutes and talk about what went wrong. Even though I had not completed the tunnel of fire successfully, I wanted to complete the show.

After completing the exit interview, the decision was made that my friends Jeff and Cory would drive me to Denver where I could see one of the top burn specialists in the country. After the six-hour drive we arrived in the early morning just in time for the doctor to look me over. He was able to clean me up and trim away some of the dead skin. He said the severity of the burns to my wrists was the most critical but that my hands and back would also require skin grafts.

I had suffered 3rd degree burns to my hands and back. Jeff and Cory set off on their flights out of town, and my girlfriend and I got tickets to fly into California to see a second burn specialist where I could get my final treatment.

After arriving in Los Angeles, my parents met up with us at a local hotel until my appointment that day at the burn center. I knew my parents were very concerned, and I will never forget the look on their faces.

As soon as I saw them, I felt even worse for putting them through something like this.

That day I started my treatment at the burn center they began cleaning up my wounds and going over the procedures needed to fix my hands and back.

Through the years I had broken quite a few bones including my shoulder blade, hand, shoulders, and foot.

The burns were by far the most painful as my nerves had been damaged. From the years of experience in hospital visits, I knew I was in for some pain on my way into the first surgery.

A PICC line was placed in my body to administer Dilaudid into my blood stream more quickly.

This was the first indication that I was in for a treat this time around. Waking up after the first surgery was more of a nightmare than anything. I had never felt pain so intense in my life. The first surgery was important to clean my hands thoroughly of all debris, which meant heavy scrubbing.

The surgeon pinned down my fingers which caused all of my nails to crack. I was cleaned up, and cadaver skin was placed on my back and hands to trick my body into cell repair. The pain was excruciating, and I remember screaming inside with agony. Then I realized that I was screaming out loud. The look of my family in front of my bed said it all.

The concern, fear, and love were there, but this pain was something I couldn't share with anyone. My nurse came in to feed Dilaudid directly into my PICC line, which took only seconds to race into my heart and throughout my bloodstream. My body would get an instant jolt that would literally make me gasp heavily. This helped alleviate the severity of the pain but was still very present

The burn center was busy, and after my surgery I had a roommate who was also burned.

I had three days until my second surgery was scheduled, so for the time being I was trying to remain strong, keep my spirits high, and rest.

On the second day my roommate began to complain about things in the room and the way the staff was treating him. It soon became apparent that this man suffered from mental illness and was acting out for unknown reasons.

Within 15 minutes of him lashing out, the nurses were trying to calm him down and accommodate. During all this commotion I could literally feel myself becoming ill. My heart rate increased and soon took over my entire body. I began to feel sick and called for a nurse. I told her,

"I think this man's negativity is making me sick!"

They quickly moved him, and the nurses sat me up to control my breathing. I had never in my life been able to see someone else's negativity directly impact my physical well-being so measurably.

From that day forward I made the decision to cut out the negativity in my life as much as possible. To this day, I still can't tolerate negative people like I used to. To a certain extent all of us have negative things or people in our lives, but for me I began to make a point to minimize this as much as possible.

The second lesson I learned was just as important as the first. Time for my second surgery had come, and this time around the doctors warned me it would be more painful than the first. Is that even possible?

I was going to have my skin taken from my legs and grafted onto my hands and back to replace the skin that had been burned off. I will give the doctor credit where due; he was right. The second surgery was more painful than the first. My thighs had literally been stripped of their skin in order to cover my back and hands.

This made it very difficult to function, let alone walk, but I was told walking was important to stay loose and active. My good friend Jon and my Aunt Nancy were there by my side taking turns visiting and keeping me company.

Day in and day out Jon made me get up and walk around the nurses' lobby. I knew I had a great friend when I would wake up and see him there visiting me and pushing me to recover.

For 11 days, I spent two hours a day in the hyperbaric oxygen chamber breathing a high concentration of oxygen that helps the body heal faster. The day after my second surgery, I was in a lot of pain and thought things couldn't get worse.

I was wrong; they could, and it was here and then I realized things can always be worse.

I slowly made my way into the oxygen room where there were two oxygen chambers. This time there was a second patient who was covered head to toe in medical wraps.

I mean, this guy looked as though he was mummified. As the nurse stepped away briefly, I looked over at him and asked,

"How are you doing, man?"

His reply was simple but will always stay with me:

"I'm doing better each day."

I began to think to myself, if this guy is covered head to toe in wraps and is in good spirits, then I really need to focus on staying positive and remember that things could, in fact, always be worse.

From that day forward I began to run those words through my head whenever things seemed grim during my recovery. Eleven days in the hospital, and then I was home recovering.

I received some great phone calls from good friends, family, and sponsors. Although not all phone calls were good. In fact, I had one sponsor not even call to check in on me, and I had another tell me it might be time for me to toss in the towel and quit riding, that I had a great run at things and had more of a career than they even thought was possible.

I remember getting off the speaker phone, as I couldn't use my hands for anything, and it was almost as if a light bulb in my head went off. This phone call spearheaded the idea for me to utilize this time to not only come back from my injuries but to come back stronger than ever before.

My family and girlfriend threw a benefit BBQ to help me get back on my feet financially, and I focused on my physical therapy. I was so motivated to come back stronger that I began to do my physical therapy six hours a day. I also began brainstorming how I would get back into my career. The idea struck me to build a different type of stunt bike than I previously had.

Until then many riders had used Japanese bikes like Kawasaki to stunt. Now I was thinking outside the box with a bold new idea. I called up my sponsors and told them my idea. I was going to build the first ever Aprilia sportbike stunt bike. They were happy to hear of my idea, but I still had a few hurdles to overcome. The most urgent was to physically recover.

Easier said than done!

7 DON'T CALL IT A COMEBACK

After my extensive surgeries I struggled each day to walk, eat, clothe myself, and change bandages.

This was definitely a low point in my life where I would have to be strong to come out on top. Laying down for bed hurt and I was getting an average of about four hours of sleep a night. I even took the liberty of getting fish to stare at while lying down so I could calm myself and distract myself from the pain.

Whatever means it took to calm my nerves and get better. That was my goal, to get better! After about one month, the legs began to bend normally, and new skin was coming in nicely.

The back was beginning to feel better, but the hands were still not functioning other than to show people I could drop just about anything I tried to pick up.

By month two, I had lined up getting the new Aprilia motorcycle. The ideas started flowing; I was not only going to build the ultimate stunt bike for next season, but I was going to document the build online and set out on a national tour performing stunts.

The goals seemed very high at the time, especially considering I couldn't even use my hands. What I quickly learned was that I do well under pressure and having goals for myself incentivized me.

Nurses, doctors, friends, family, or sponsors can only do so much, but I learned to give myself goals in order to make the recovery more manageable.

My first goal was to gain mobility in my hands, but what would I do for myself mentally?

The goal to build the ultimate bike and go on national tour was the ticket I needed to focus and keep the mind occupied from the obvious day-to-day struggles with pain and frustration.

By the third month, the bike had arrived, and I was able to get it up to my place.

My hands were still wrapped with bandages, but having the bike there motivated me to keep up with my physical therapy so that I could use my hands on any level to start work on the bike.

As I began working on the bike, my hands started bleeding. It felt like forever, but really it had been four months since my incident. My hands were not quite ready to be used, but mentally I couldn't take the wait any longer. I slowly began taking apart the new motorcycle, and a job that should have taken me an hour to do would turn into a weeklong project as my hands had no strength and very little mobility.

My father had a hot rod shop next door, and he would come by to check on me from time to time. He would get upset when he would see my bandages red from the blood coming through.

After weeks of working on the motorcycle, I soon shifted my attention to also getting rid of the weight I gained from sitting on my butt for months.

I bought a bicycle and walked the bike outside my place. I figured this would be the first step to getting back on a motorcycle. I walked the bike over to a bicycle trail where nobody could watch, as I knew this was going to be a sight to see. I could barely get my hands around the bars let alone ride well.

As I picked up a little momentum, I began to straighten out a bit and feel the breeze against my face. The breeze felt amazing and literally lifted my spirits with each pedal of the bike. Something as simple as riding a bicycle had lifted my spirits up, not so much for the fact that I could ride a bicycle but because it confirmed the idea that I could come back even stronger if I devoted myself to it.

Only a few hundred yards into this bike ride, and I felt as if I had covered 10 miles. My hands were not holding onto the bars anymore, and my lungs were coughing up all the junk from not exercising. I had to walk the bike home, but I did so with my chin up and a grin on my face. The trick was to not just come back into my old self but to come back even stronger.

The bicycle became an obsession for me.

How long could I travel today, and how strong was I compared to the previous day?

Not only was I training, but I was also building the most beautiful bike I had ever built. My build was becoming well known within the Aprilia Sportbike community, and throughout the build I was documenting it with step-by-step photos. Soon the build had reached 40,000 viewers, and then one day I received a call from Aprilia USA.

They liked my build and gave me some tips for what to do on the electronics and braking components. I was building a small amount of momentum with the bike, physical therapy, and sponsors. About a month into the build, I was nearly finished and wanted to make sure that when the bike was unveiled it would receive the attention it deserved.

I had my friend Andrew Carpenter come down from Washington and photograph it with his style of photography. He has an amazing eye for photographing motorcycles, and since he had a similar bike himself, he knew how to capture the beauty just right.

Within the first day of shooting, Andrew sent the photos to his friend in England who immediately got it featured on the largest motorcycle Instagram pages. From that day forward it became known as one of the best-looking Aprilias out there.

Now that the bike was complete, it was time to focus my attention on practicing and setting up shows for the new year. The practicing was off to a very slow start with not only having to get used to my hands but also becoming accustomed to an entirely new style of motorcycle.

I can usually jump from one bike to the next with a few days of practice before I get entirely accustomed to the bike. This bike was an entirely different beast than what I was used to and therefore took a lot longer to tame.

For 2014, I wanted to come up with a different schedule of events than I had ever done before or a different route of doing them. I came up with the idea to go on a national tour for the summer and perform at some of the largest motorcycle dealers throughout the Midwest and East Coast. After a few weeks of my sponsors deliberating on the issue, I finally got the green light.

Their concerns were valid, as I had just been through a lot over the previous months. I had a few things going for me that I pointed out to them. One of them being that I had been on board with my sponsors for over seven years and was determined to come back strong.

I wanted to show them the same results, if not more, than I had throughout the previous years. This was a huge motivation for me to have a great year. I was not only going to get back on the motorcycle, but I was going to set out to have one of my best years yet.

I had a month before I was to set out on this summer tour, and I was doing my best to get healthy and more accustomed to the bike.

As I beat the bikes I perform on pretty harshly, I knew I needed a backup bike for the tour. I didn't want to be across the country performing and have a break down and not be able to perform.

So I went with my favorite brand and purchased a Kawasaki Zx6, which is known for its reliability and power. My second task was to find a pretty woman to help during my tour.

I called my friend Kellie, and she was jumping at the chance to help. By the end of the day, she had given her two-week notice at work.

Next thing I did was purchase a van to stash the motorcycles in for traveling across the country. It wasn't much to look at, but it was a step in the right direction. I will always remember the conversation Kellie and I had before we left for the trip. We promised each other we would do our best to stay positive and that there would be highs and lows during the trip but to not forget that we had the opportunity of a lifetime to travel and have fun. That agreement was one of the best things we did as the tour challenged both of us physically and mentally over the 63 days across the country.

Our first performance was scheduled for Kansas City, Missouri, and this being the first of 25 events over the course of two months, I was very anxious to see how this whole thing would play out. My hands were, of course, a huge concern, as holding onto the 400 lb. bike while performing was of the upmost importance. The booth was set up, the posters were being autographed, but now the time had come to perform.

As I began putting on my jacket and gloves, I could feel a boost of adrenaline surge throughout my body. As I strapped on my helmet, it felt like I hadn't skipped a beat. There wasn't anything left to do but to perform. Missouri weather kicked in, and half way into my show it started raining. As a general rule of riding professionally, I will continue to perform as long as the spectators stay to watch. Nobody got up to leave, so I finished my 20-minute show in the rain. I was back, and it felt so sweet!

Over the next couple weeks my promotional model and I started getting into a groove of setting up the booth, performing, and traveling from city to city while at the same time reminding ourselves to have fun when given the chance and especially to seek out fun when morale was low.

One of the not-so-high points of the trip was when, while in Illinois, we stopped by the famous "cloud."

After taking some photos and videos for sponsors, we headed west to a small shop in Chicago. While on the highway, the van began to billow out a large amount of smoke from the passenger side. Pulling off the highway, I determined that the front right brake had seized and was not allowing the front tire to freely spin. I was upset as we only had 40 minutes before we were scheduled to arrive for the show. As I was under the van, Kellie kicked my feet, started laughing, and took a photo of me. I pulled out from under the van and was not happy with what was going on, but as I looked up at her and saw her laughing with that smile on her face, I remembered the promise we made to each other at the beginning of the trip. Have fun even during the rough times. I began to laugh at the situation and relaxed for a moment. I remembered my dad teaching me a trick when I was a young kid with my dirt bike. I got right back under the van and within a minute, patched up the van good enough to limp to the next event.

After that performance I worked on the van to completely fix the brake issues. It had to get done because our next stop was Ohio for one of the largest motorcycle dealers in the nation.

Exhausted after driving all day, we crashed for the night.

The next day we arrived in Ohio, and we pulled a six-hour day at the shop. I was exhausted, and my body began to feel like it would never stop being sore. After we packed up that night, Kellie and I discussed the idea of stopping by Niagara Falls since we had two days off before our next show.

We set out for an early start the next morning and got caught in a huge rainstorm that made our trip to Niagara an entire day's drive. Not feeling like doing much that night, I pulled up to the hotel. All I wanted to do was take a hot shower and bunker in for the night, but Kellie had slept most the trip there, so she was full of energy. She convinced me to put off my shower and head down to the falls. As we made our way to the falls, it was dark, but I started to hear water bouncing off the rocks. As we fought for positioning against the fence, I looked over and saw an amazing spectacle, the falls in all their glory. Anyone who has been there would know what I am talking about–the evening light bouncing off the mist, the sound of the water bouncing from the rocks, and the beauty of nature herself. Here in this moment, I recognized not only how lucky I was to be at the falls sharing a moment with a friend, but also the fact that only six months previously I had been in a serious accident and nearly met my demise.

Within seconds of that thought, a fireworks show started to erupt, and the spectacle I had just been in awe of just got even more exciting. This was truly a moment I would never forget.

Kellie and I had a three-day layover in Indiana, and I made use of the time to fix one of the radiators that exploded on one of the bikes. My good friend SIC Nate back in California was nice enough to find me a new radiator and ship it out. I was also fortunate enough to have met another aspiring stunt rider in town and used his garage to work on the bikes. He asked that in return I head out to the local stunt spot and give him a few pointers on his riding. As I have been riding for years, I have been asked many times to help people with their riding.

I have always been a little nervous as this sport has a drastic learning curve, and it can go from right to wrong very quickly with little forgiveness. A man of my word, I promised Eddie I would teach him a few things and give him some pointers on how to become a better rider. As I began unloading, Eddie was excited and had already slapped on his riding gear and began practicing. I could see he was anxious to show me his skill level, and it was nice to see his enthusiasm.

Right away I saw some things that made me nervous. As I was putting my gear on to catch up to Eddie and say something, I heard the sound that any rider recognizes without having to look. It was the sound of metal grinding against the ground and plastic snapping into pieces. As I turned around, I could see the motorcycle flipping straight back on its tail with the front wheel pointed straight up in the air while Eddie tumbled head over heels. The motorcycle took a pretty hard hit, but Eddie seemed to get the worst of it. As I rushed over to check on him, he was ok, but it looked as though he had just separated his shoulder.

After being released from the hospital, it turned out that he had also suffered a broken collarbone. I was only staying a few houses down from where Eddie lived, so Kellie came up with the idea to do something nice for him. Kellie immediately went to the store and got groceries to surprise Eddie and his girlfriend with a home-cooked meal so that when they got home from the hospital they wouldn't have to worry about dinner.

As I picked Eddie and his girlfriend up at the hospital, I told them Kellie was up to something at the house. When we arrived, Kellie had made an amazing meal, and I remember thinking Kellie was growing up as this trip progressed.

This trip was becoming much more than just work and fun; it was also allowing Kellie to grow into herself.

Thirteen events into the tour Kellie and I found ourselves in New York City during the Fourth of July. We could stay on Staten Island with a few friends, or we could live it up and lure our friends to join us in the city. Another moment like Niagara Falls came into mind. Taking the ferry from Staten Island to the city, I was sitting at the top of the ferry with the sun setting at my back and a cold beer in my hand. The sunset was bouncing off the Atlantic Ocean, and the Statue of liberty looked ever-so-impressive standing tall. That night Kellie and I watched the fireworks up close and personal with the Brooklyn Bridge and three barges setting off fireworks. This was the largest fireworks show I had ever seen, and here I was with another night I would never forget.

As the tour came closer to being complete, Kellie and I found ourselves taking advantage of every scenario we could.

We saw monuments, rode jet skis, did a photoshoot on a subway platform, and tried unique restaurants and bars.

I was riding so much that soon my body wasn't sore anymore. Our second-to-last stop was New Orleans, and this was not a stop for business but solely pleasure. I had heard so much about this city and the party scene it had to offer.

I don't consider myself a party animal, but I have certainly been to my fair share of parties over my career. We shacked up at a nice hotel in the French Quarter in downtown New Orleans.

We were hungry and tired from the long trip straight from North Carolina but weren't going to let that keep us in for the night. We showered up and headed out for what life had to offer. It was a Friday night, and things were going off–music, dancing, restaurants, drinking, art shows, you name it. First things first as we sat down to eat and consume adult beverages.

Kellie and I had only a week left on this trip, and we were going to pack it in with as much fun as we possibly could. What better place to give it a try than New Orleans. After one of the best meals of my life, we walked around the late night art show. We then found ourselves making our way to a bar that had live music. What we quickly learned was that every bar in the French Quarter seemed to have live music.

Drink after drink we found ourselves walking from each bar to the next, and the party literally wouldn't stop. Either we were sweating the liquor out from the dancing and bar hopping or it was the jumbo shrimp soaking it all up. Every bar felt like it was welcoming you in for the best time of your life. With nearly 6,000 miles logged and only one show left for the tour, Kellie and I were determined to live it up. On the way back to the hotel, there were three of us walking.

I had met a fine young lady who was enjoying the night as much as I was, and better yet, we were enjoying each other's company. Kellie gave us some time alone in the room, and by 3 am my lady friend and I found ourselves outside the balcony that night in the buff.

For tonight, I was living in the moment.

8 HATERS

Keyboard warriors, Internet gangsters — I thought about leaving out the haters in my life, but then I began to think about where my life would be without the hate.

Sure, I may be a lot happier and think more positively about the general public, but on the other hand, haters provide little reminders for me to do my very best. If my fans, family, and sponsors always told me that I am the best and never gave me any constructive criticism, then I would go on riding on the same level and think I am the best. It's the haters, keyboard warriors, and Internet gangsters that keep me grounded and searching to prove them wrong.

Perhaps it's best to share an example from the recent past. In 2011, a new trick had just come out. It entailed stalling the motorcycle during a wheelie and while the bike was completely still, jumping as much as I can into a superman-like position, meaning my feet leap out from underneath while the bike is standing still in a wheelie. I was one of the first to successfully complete this stunt here in the United States, and my sponsors were the first to come out with two-page print in a magazine with the shot. The photo was voted Best Motorcycle Ad for 2011, and I was happy along with my sponsors. Soon after, I began to hear that the photo was great but that there was no way I had landed that trick. This began to bother me, which it shouldn't have.

Why would I need to prove myself to everyone? I only needed to prove anything to my sponsors and self. I came up with the idea to not only film the trick but to perform it with style and a more dramatic setting. The idea was to film me performing the trick against a semi truck. I called in a favor to a friend to get his nice camera and assistant, and we headed to find a semi truck parked somewhere we could film.

After setting up the cameras and warming up a bit, I decided to go for it. After about 10 minutes I started to get frustrated. Why was I having such a hard time?

I had introduced a semi into the trick, and it was causing issues with the stunt. I could no longer just flick my legs back superman-style into the air. Now, I had to calculate how close I would need to be in order to safely plant my feet against the semi but not so close that I jammed myself up and fell eight feet face first. I was literally there for an hour before I landed the stunt to my standard. My motivation for this trick was not for another magazine print but the satisfaction of knowing I would at least show a few of my haters out there that I could in fact perform this trick, and I would have to go out of my way to prove it.

The video went on to do well on all social media platforms, but the satisfaction for me was showing myself and others that it could be done.

Fast forwarding to 2014, I was on a national tour performing at 25 shops. During my second stop of the tour one of the shops informed me that they had liked my video that my sponsor had put out. I was not aware of any video being televised at motorcycle shops about me. Moments later he pointed up to the TV playing inside the shop. There I was jumping against a semi. As it turns out, my sponsor BikeMaster had put together an advertising clip of my trial and error with the new semi stunt. I stood there and had a huge grin on my face. To think that, if it wasn't for the haters, I may have never tried to video the stunt and would have never made it into an advertising clip that had obviously stood out to my sponsor as being unique.

This doesn't mean having negative people in your life or reading negative things about you is good. I just remember to take it with a grain of salt even though sometimes it's hard for us to let it go. Not everyone is going to like you, especially when they don't like themselves or their lives. There are those of us who get up in the morning and take on the day, and there are those who let the day pass them by. Who do you want to be?

9 ONLY SO MUCH

I was in Northern California at Sonoma Raceway for the NHRA drag races and what made this day special was the fact Jon, my good friend, had made the six-hour drive with me to watch me perform over the weekend.

We arrived a day early so we could visit the local town in which we went to college, go to our favorite restaurant, and visit bars in the evening. We also met up with a few more friends that still lived in the Santa Rosa area.

Jon was going to law school while my buddy Matt had taken a position at a Marin Range Rover dealership.

Matt's sister, Melissa, was a special education teacher at a local school.

It was obvious what I had been up to over the years since college. I had been riding for the past six years and was currently trying to land a new sponsor. I was explaining to everyone that sponsors are like girlfriends. In theory, the more the merrier. However, to a certain extent, the more sponsors you have the more responsibility and pressure you have to please each one. I have been lucky to have three sponsors over the years that show me support: Dunlop, Speed & Strength, and BikeMaster.

This year, I was looking to include Geico as a new sponsor. I had been performing all year for the NHRA drag races and alongside my performances, there was always a Geico sponsored promotional team who shot T-shirts into the crowd and announced during my stunt shows. This had been going on for months now and I had the idea it would be even better if I was representing Geico on my bike.

I explained to my friends over dinner that I had worked my way up the ladder with them and was scheduled to meet with a member of the company at the event this weekend. We decided to call it an early night as Jon and I had to be up early for the event.

By 7 am the next morning, we were up and heading to the track. We already had the motorcycles and trailer at the event and just needed to park the truck and meet up with a local promotional model to help at the booth for the day. As I arrived at the trailer and began unpacking, my promotional model showed up looking amazing. Jon was excited to help out and was lending a hand setting things up and ensuring the booth looked its best.

The spot we got couldn't have been better, as we were closest to the track. I could walk my bike up to the performance area and the spectator traffic funneled right through our booth. Along with our trackside location, we managed to be placed no further than 50 feet from the Geico booth. By 11 am, we were receiving a lot of spectator traffic and selling a lot of shirts. My contact at Geico came by and wished me good luck with my 12 o'clock performance. He said he would be watching with the boss and would like to speak with me after.

I don't get nervous before a performance, but as I began to walk my bike over to the performance area I explained to Jon that this performance had to be high energy with no faults. I was feeling the pressure to put on a great show.

The track official began calling my name and introducing me to the crowd. Jon slapped the side of my helmet and told me to knock 'em dead! As I fired up the bike and sped onto the track, I looked up and saw 10,000 spectators to my left and another 5,000 to my right.

It was time for me to shine. Before this moment, it had taken me six months to get the contact at Geico, another month of emailing, and another month to set up the meeting.

I had taken the time to draw up my ideas for us to work together and made a very nice proposal for them to evaluate. So here I was, finally at the time where I could show not only the race fans what I could do, but also a potential sponsor who was literally in the stands watching me.

I focused on delivering a clean performance with high energy. For the next 10 minutes, I was racing up and down the performance area, throwing in all the newest and best tricks I knew.

I put together a high energy routine with some of the newer tricks I had been practicing recently. I felt like I had pounded an energy drink in five seconds.

My heart was racing and I could feel my chest pounding up and down from breathing so heavily. I was putting everything I had into this show and my body was feeling the effects. It was nearly 90 degrees out and with the bike between my legs, I was sweating like a pig. I could hear the spectators cheering and feel the energy from the crowd, which made me ride even harder.

I looked over at the Geico announcer giving me the signal that one minute was left. As I came down the track, I looked to my left and right and saw people standing up and cheering for me. No matter how many times I see spectators cheering, it always makes me feel invincible. So many things go into these performances: the practice, the driving, the maintenance, the crashes, and the hospital visits.

It's moments like this that make it all worth it.

As I pulled up to the booth, I saw a crowd already forming. I handed the bike over to Jon and I started signing posters.

About an hour later, my Geico contact tells me that, when I get chance, I should come by the RV and have a talk with him. I headed over after I signed my last poster and was excited to finally have a chance to give him my pitch.

I sat down in the RV and thanked him for his time. He was impressed with my performance and wanted to hear my thoughts for my relationship with Geico. The NHRA drag races have me perform during the event and with 20,000 spectators watching me, it made sense to combine Geico with myself. My thoughts were that the Geico promotional show would include a Geico-sponsored rider performing in front of motorsports enthusiasts.

After I said what I needed to say, he began to ask questions.

Why is my booth so small? And why don't I have a bigger set up than my 15 foot trailer?

It was a bit of a slap in the face, but I always try to remember not to take things personally. I had gotten this far from the support of my existing sponsors and each year, I try to better myself and my presence at events. My sponsors have done a lot for me, providing my rig, bikes, clothing, bike parts, and my salary. I told him I was looking for a sponsor like Geico that would like to capitalize on the exposure I receive from all the different types of events in which I perform.

He was not easy to read, and I wasn't sure what to make of the interview besides the fact I said what I was there to say and I performed to the best of my ability. The fact that I was able to get the meeting and come this far was nice, but I was looking to seal the deal and team up for next year. He informed me that he would think things over and discuss it with his team.

Later that evening, Jon and I packed everything up and headed out to get dinner. He asked me how things went with the meeting and I told him it went well from my perspective, but that I would be hearing back from them within the week.

We stopped by one of our favorite college spots to eat.

Over dinner, we discussed how far we each have come since college. Jon was going to law school and I was riding sportbikes professionally. I felt very fortunate to be where I was at that moment in life.

With our bellies full, vehicle gassed, and music playing, Jon and I headed back home.

Being home for a week seemed like an eternity. It felt like I was waiting for my SAT score in high school. Except this time, it was me waiting to see if I had landed a big sponsor for next year.

On day eight of waiting, I received an email from my contact at Geico. It read,

"after further evaluation and review we respectfully decline your proposal".

Within seconds, my day went from good to bad and there was nothing I could do about it. I had spent months on this project and put a lot of time and effort into being professional on and off the track. I remember looking out the window and thinking how could they turn down such an opportunity?

I wasn't asking for much and I certainly showed them what I could do. Was I asking for too much money? Was my performance not what they expected? Was my booth not up to their standards? I could have sat there and asked myself questions until late in the evening. I didn't. I got up and went for a walk. I just let myself take it in for a while and began to remind myself that life can get a lot worse than being turned down. This was business, not personal, and I tried to remember that.

The first person I called was Jon, and he was shocked. He had witnessed my efforts and has seen what I can bring to the table for all my sponsors throughout the years.

After some kind words of encouragement, I decided there was really nothing further I could do.

A lesson was learned that day. I can try as hard as I can and want something badly, but that doesn't make it happen. The point is that I tried. You can't hit the ball if you don't swing.

10 CRAZY WEEKEND

Have you ever been in the middle of an interview and realized that the person interviewing you was on drugs? I sure have, and it was as awkward as it sounds.

Over the course of my riding career, I have done many interviews for radio, TV, and print. They don't always go as planned, but for the most part I have learned to have fun with them and speak the truth. Truth be told, I was in San Diego doing a TV spot on a local news channel to help promote an open house event at a motorcycle shop. It was 7 am, and I was asked to interview with a local TV host and perform a few stunts during the live interview.

Before we went live, the host was sweating profusely and speaking a million miles an hour. He was fumbling to complete a sentence and was making everyone around him uneasy. Off air he asked me a few questions about myself and if I would be willing to do a few wheelies around him and two Hooters girls once they went live.

I explained to him that doing wheelies in general is dangerous and that I would not feel comfortable doing them around three people I didn't know while live on TV.

He began to get upset at me and asked me if I was a professional or an amateur. He obviously thought that insulting me would get him places, but like I said before, we didn't know each other, and he didn't know who he just insulted. After talking it over with the motorcycle shop and sound guys, they agreed that all it would take was for one of the girls or the host to step in front of me and bad things could happen. I explained to everyone that my sponsors would not like to see Clint take out two Hooters girls on live TV.

By now the host was very irritated due to the fact he wanted a specific shot and began talking down about my skill level. I obviously couldn't assault the man as my sponsors were watching, and I couldn't verbally insult him as I wouldn't lower myself to his level.

So as he began to start his interview broadcasting live from San Diego with two beautiful women by his side, I decided to come in from out of frame and just start riding and making a bunch of noise so nobody could hear him. In my head this was a great decision, but in hindsight maybe it wasn't the most mature thing to do. It was too late.

I was already on the bike zipping back and forth behind him for 20 seconds, messing around, and ended with a burnout. Needless to say, he lost his train of thought and was outraged. As they went to commercial, he stormed over to me and yelled about how horrible that went.

He threw down his microphone and stormed off to the news van.

My sponsor walked over to me and asked what I was doing. My reply was simple: "I couldn't be disrespected like that. You guys hire me to represent you because of who I am, and you just got to see who I am when confronted by a TV host on drugs."

The funny part was that this was just the start of a long weekend.

The next evening another rider and I were hired to perform at Pepperdine University in Malibu. This was definitely going to be a first for me since I had never performed at a pep rally before. Sure, in high school I had been to my fair share of them, but I never thought I would be performing at one.

I am used to performing for motorsports enthusiasts, and this show was anything but that. It was a basketball rally that included Red Bull girls handing out drinks, free hot dogs and burgers, music, and of course the stunt show. Before most events, we usually do a meet and greet as well as sign posters and have our promotional model hand out free stickers and hats.

Things were already starting off awkwardly with the music being a bit low energy and low volume for our liking. Students were walking around not sure what to make of us, and very few of them made it to our table to say hello. We had two performances that night, so we decided to break the ice and get the first show started a bit early.

We put on our own music and began warming up the bikes. Our promotional girl got on the microphone to introduce us to everyone and tell them what it is that we do.

We started off the show with a few burnouts then wheelies, but half way into the show I began to notice these students were either not impressed with what we were doing or didn't know how to show their enthusiasm. Either way, when the spectators are not into the performance, it really doesn't get me in the mood to perform at my best and is a buzzkill for sure.

My buddy and I looked at each other and could clearly read the situation.

We needed to step up our energy in order to really get a reaction. We began to perform more difficult maneuvers and faster-paced tricks.

After 25 minutes of performing we shut down the bikes over next to the booth. The students were not coming over to say hello, they were not asking for photos, and they certainly didn't clap in enthusiasm.

My buddy and I were dumbfounded. I had never in my career had such a strange response to a performance. I understand that I was not shooting a rocket into space, but we were performing some dangerous tricks on motorcycles at a University.

You'd think we would at least get the students excited to see something different. After a few kids came over and said hello, my buddy and I couldn't understand what was happening when the event coordinator for the University came over and seemed very pleased.

He commented on how much he liked the performance, but we voiced our concern about the students' lack of enthusiasm for the show. He said he heard students walking away from the show say that it was great and that they couldn't wait for the second performance and that the students mostly likely didn't know how to react.

In his opinion we were doing fine. Just fine!? I don't perform just fine. I perform at a high level of energy, and in return the spectators feed off my energy. So I guessed this meant we needed to step things up for our next show because I was definitely not leaving that place until I felt we did our best and gave those students something to cheer for.

During the 45-minute break my buddy and I began to think over how we could change up our routine in order to increase the excitement.

The main problem had to do with the amount of space we had to perform in. Usually, the more space provided, the more speed and stunts for us to perform. This, in return, increases the energy and excitement during the performance.

We were limited to about a 150-foot area but were set on doing something different to mix things up. After students had finished eating, they headed back over to the performance area. We told our promotional model to really yell into the microphone and get these students fired up. It certainly couldn't hurt that she had changed wardrobe into a short skirt, cute top, and high heels. It was about 8 pm, and the sun was down. My buddy and I began a routine of a more synchronized set of tricks. We performed circle wheelies side by side, high revving burnouts side by side, and even drifted around our promotional model to add a bit of excitement. The kids were definitely more into the show with some light cheers. That is when things literally began to heat up! It was as if the low energy was upsetting my buddy, and at that moment he decided to take matters into his own hands. He jumped off his bike and headed over to the booth where he picked up our gas can that we use to fill up the bikes.

He walked it over to the middle of the performance area and dumped what seemed to be a gallon of gas on the ground. He slid the can back over to the booth and pulled out a lighter from his pants. He tossed the lighter directly on top of the puddle of gas, and "BOOM" — she lit up like a Christmas tree! I couldn't believe he just did that! Were we going to get kicked out of there or arrested? It was likely one of the two. Well, if we were, we might as well go out in style. We went on with the show and did wheelies through and around the fire. As we began to get tired, we noticed the kids were definitely at their most excited. We finished the show, and the kids stood still as if the show wasn't done. I decided to take off my helmet and ride around the performance barricade to slap high fives with the students. I was getting the feedback I wanted now. I was ending this performance on a personal note. In a way I was saying thanks for sticking around to watch us. After completing my lap around the barricade saying thanks, I saw the students begin to make their way over to our booth.

We considered ourselves somewhat successful and learned a few things along the way. From that performance on, I have always concluded my shows with a round of high fives.

We packed up that evening and talked about how strange that was in comparison to other events we had done in the past. We had little time to relax as we had just a few hours of sleep to rest then off to Arizona for the third and final show of the week.

The last two performances were a bit strange so I was looking forward to performing at Hot Import Nights since we had performed for this car show before.

Hot Import Nights was an all-out party that had import cars, import models, and live entertainment including drift cars and stunt riders. Basically, the best way to describe it was an event to overload the senses.

The upside to this event was that we had performed at these before and knew this would be a great crowd to perform in front of. After a few hours of sleep, we left Los Angeles and headed out to Arizona. Seven hours into the desert we made our way to Firebird Raceway. We had arrived an hour or so early so decided to take a short nap in the rig. We were wiped out, and I was especially tired since this was my third event in three days. Not only was I tired, but my bike was getting worked pretty hard as well. Went through two rear tires already, and I was sure to go through another tonight. After a quick nap, a good meal, and an energy drink, I was ready to take on the last event of the weekend.

The gates opened to the performers at 4 pm, and we headed in to set up the booth and bikes for the night's performances. It was nearly 5 pm and was 90 degrees with no sign of it cooling down much. As the sun started to drop, the gates opened to the public, and the entertainment began.

We had two performances that night, and the first one started at 8 pm. By 7:30 the event was packed with attendance higher than I had seen in a while. Models were walking around taking pictures with import cars, live DJs were playing music, and the drift cars were out laying rubber down for the spectators.

My buddy and I began warming up the bikes and putting on our gear as our promotional model came out of the rig wearing a short skirt, stripper heels, fishnets, and a pink top. I remember thinking, what the hell is going on?! She had a new look in order to step up her game around all these other beautiful women.

After the drifters were done, our names were called up and announced for the show. We were given 30 minutes to perform and were excited to get out there. We had a huge performance area but decided to concentrate most of our stunts close to the fence and perform at opposite ends of the track in order to entertain the full length of spectators.

We zig zagged back and forth from one end of the fence to the other with a high amount of energy since this crowd was expecting a great show. With high-speed drifting, burnouts, and fast wheelies, this crowd was definitely into it. The more excited the crowd got, the more adrenaline surged through my body. After 25 minutes we were getting tired from the heat, and the bikes began to overheat as well. We decided to come in early and let a few of our friends on smaller bikes go out and do their thing.

Taking off my helmet, I had sweat dripping down my face, and my jacket felt like a sponge.

I needed to cool down quickly and hydrate. That performance went very well, and the crowd already began surging around the booth. We were taking pictures with spectators, signing posters, and having a blast. Our booth was busy for the next hour. This was the kind of show we wanted and definitely could use after the previous two.

We had about an hour before our last performance at 11 pm, and it was still hot in the Arizona desert.

My buddy and I strategized how our next performance would go. We wanted to change things up a bit and also include our promotional model. We decided to let our friends head out on the small bikes first to hype up the crowd. We put in our own music to drown out the background music played by the DJ. We wanted our last performance of the night to bring the most people from around the event over to our area and show everyone what sportbike freestyle is about. As our friends finished up their 10-minute routine, my buddy and I fired up our bikes.

With microphone in hand, heels on, and skirt riding high, our promotional model walked out to the performance area to gain full attention. With that outfit I believe she got all the attention she needed. She announced us to the crowd and as planned, the music started blasting, and we shot off like cannons. As discussed earlier, we didn't want the show to drag on. We wanted to ride to the best of our ability and with high energy even if that meant sacrificing the longevity of the show.

In order to make sure this occurred, we both shotgunned an energy drink minutes before we went out. To say the least, we were more than excited to get out there. The motorcycles were screaming that night, and our tires were dragging rubber all across the concrete. My buddy and I were riding flawlessly and feeding off the energy of not only the crowd but each other. Twenty minutes into the performance, and I was beginning to feel fatigue in my arms. I had "arm pump", which meant my forearms were swelling up, and I was having a hard time holding onto the bars. I was spent for the night, and my father always told me only bad things happen when you're tired on a motorcycle.

I ended the show with a huge burnout and popped my rear tire. Spectators shouted in appreciation, and it felt as if the air that night was electric...although it was probably just a side effect of the energy drink.

After the show we received another wave of spectators that came by to say hi, take photos, and get some free stuff at the booth. It was a great night, and we had successfully ended this three-day performance week on a high note. As the crowd around the booth began to thin out, my buddy and I decided to sit at the side of the performance area on the guard rail and just take some time to ourselves and relax. Sitting on top of the concrete barrier and taking in the evening was a nice break that lasted all of two minutes before a camera crew and two beautiful girls came our way.

When I say beautiful, I mean to say half-dressed ladies who looked like they just got off work at a strip club.

I wasn't too far off when they told us they were impressed by our riding and had a question for me. One of the girls told me that she works with a specific porn site and currently does porn for a living. She asked if I would be willing to tape a scene in our rig with two girls, the bike, and film crew. I knew they were serious because they had a look on their faces that was all business with a bit of pleasure. I couldn't believe they would even ask me since I was sitting on the barricade drenched in sweat and probably didn't smell all that good.

The first thing that popped into my mind was what a crazy request and that this would be like every guys dream except for the fact that I would be filmed. I told them thank you for asking, but I wouldn't be able to do something like that. Not five seconds later they stepped a few feet over to the side and asked the same thing of my buddy.

Wow, did they just do that?

It almost didn't matter who they wanted, but the scene itself was what they were looking for. One of our buddies who rode the smaller bikes spoke up behind everyone and offered his services. The ladies turned him down immediately.

Just when we thought we were done with the whole situation, our promotional model spoke up and offered her services. She said it was something she had never done and would be willing to try. What the hell was going on around here? My buddy and I just got done putting on one hell of a show and now were being asked to star in a porn video? They asked us if they could at least use the rig to film inside, and since it was my buddy's, he gave them permission.

While my friend and I packed up the booth and took care of the bikes, we stayed clear of the inside of the rig. After 20 minutes or so, they were done filming, and I honestly couldn't look our promotional girl in the eyes. She looked like she just got off a rollercoaster ride.

We loaded up the bikes and the equipment then headed to our hotel for the night. All three of us were exhausted and went to bed after our promotional model filled us in on her experience. The next morning the first thing I heard was banging on our door. Over and over again, but nobody was getting up. Housekeeping! I remember opening my eyes and seeing our promotional model get out of bed and walk over to the door nude.

She opened the door and yelled,

"What!?"

The cleaning staff stood there in shock, and one of them quietly replied, "We are here to clean, and it's past checkout." Our promotional girl swung the door all the way open and stood there with one hand on her waist and the other on the knob and said,

"Charge us another day" and slammed the door.

While lying in bed, I began to think that those past few days were some of the strangest times I had had in a while. Could this be a one-time thing, or would my stunt riding career be filled with these types of uncontrollable, sporadic, and crazy scenarios? Nah, there's no way this kind of stuff would happen all the time.

11 SMALL IMPACT

Gunfire rang out, and I almost couldn't believe what I was hearing, but growing up in a family who shot guns at the range, I knew what I heard.

What made it alarming was the fact that I wasn't at the gun range but in Watts, California performing for a charity event that was held by the city and nearby church community. This was my second year putting on a performance for the community, and although it was a rough area, I had never heard or saw any violence.

Another rider and I had just completed a performance and were handing out free shirts, hats, stickers, and signed posters to the local kids and parents when we heard the shots.

Within minutes, a helicopter was overheard looking for the suspect. It turns out the police were in search of a nearby suspect who robbed a local store. The crazier part of it to me was the fact that the local residents didn't seem concerned or alarmed.

This was something that they were used to, so I quickly went back to signing posters and handing out free stuff. The pastor in charge of the event came over to the other rider and myself and informed us that a police officer had been shot while searching for the suspect but was fortunately wearing a bulletproof vest.

This charity event went from fun to serious quickly, and after talking it over for a minute, we came to the conclusion that, although the situation was serious, the kids came out to see us ride, and that's just what we were going to do.

We stunted up and down the street stalling on fences and doing burnouts and wheelies close to the kids to make the experience all the more exciting.

After the performance I thanked everyone for coming out and began packing everything up. While I was loading my bikes, a young kid came up to me with his friends and asked for some more stickers. I gave them what I had and told them to have fun and do well in school. His reply shocked me:

"We don't go to school."

Did this kid just tell me he doesn't go to school?

I asked them if they were being honest, and all of them replied with,

"Sometimes we go, sometimes we don't."

I began to think, "How much effect do I really have on these kids? Am I doing a service of any kind by driving down here and performing, or am I just entertaining them for the day?"

After we got out of town, my friend, promotional model, and I stopped for lunch. We sat down and discussed the craziness of the day and what effect, if any, we had on these kids and the community. I'm all for helping, but I wasn't sure my presence helped in any way.

A few years later I found myself driving down to Los Angeles thinking of what I would be saying to 900 kids in junior high. I had been asked to be a guest speaker during Career Day and speak directly with the students in regards to careers and education.

I began by introducing myself and told them a little about what I do as a professional freestyle rider and experiences I have had. I spoke about education and how it has allowed me to use things I learned in school and apply it to my riding career and ultimately my life. After answering a few questions from the students, I was asked a very unique question:

"Is there any further you can go with your career choice?"

I stood there thinking of how to answer a question like this. I am my own boss, and I work as hard as I want to work. I started to think of the bike as much more than just a motorcycle.

It's more than just Clint Ewing doing stunts. Then it hit me!

My bikes allow me to do things that normally I wouldn't or couldn't do.

They have allowed me to set a world record, travel across the country, meet all types of people, and test myself physically and mentally in addition to maintaining an exciting life. There are, of course, downfalls, but overall the rewards are a much greater return.

So, here I was trying to explain myself to the kids and why I ride for a living.

I couldn't think of a better way to summarize other than to let them know that no matter what it is you choose to do with your life and your profession, try to enjoy it and give it your best because if you can give those two things, you may just end up really happy with yourself.

After the kids made their rounds talking to other speakers such as a cop, doctor, engineer, and politician, I wasn't sure my profession would be the most memorable and like in most of the things I do, I like to stand out a bit. So after the kids had a chance to meet everyone, I suited up and started the bike to put on a show.

12 PASSION

It has been 10 years since the start of my stunt riding career, and I have ended up where I least expected—or should I say I don't quite know where I am?

This is no fairy-tale ending with a house, wife, and kids. My career has literally taken me on the adventure of a lifetime. From TV appearances to traveling and meeting all types of people, I have experienced more than I could ever have imagined. I am often asked when will I stop riding and settle down with a real job. I have a real job, and I have worked very hard to be where I am today. What are any of us truly searching for, anyway?

I remember a conversation I once had that has stuck in my mind ever since. A family friend, Mr. Sampas, has three sons who are around my age. All three of them have impressive career achievements. The youngest has obtained a CPA license, a master's degree, and most recently a law degree. I congratulated Mr. Sampas for his sons' success, and his response struck me as a piece of wisdom that is obvious yet overlooked much of the time.

"I appreciate that, Clint, but what good are titles if my sons are not happy?"

I sat there for a moment and let it sink in. He is right!

What good is it to chase dreams, goals, and job titles if, in the end, you are not happy? I am guilty of it from time to time, working hard for a new sponsor or a new bike with the goal of making myself happy, when really it's the small moments in my life that carry my greatest happiness.

There are certainly moments I cherish, and one of them was just delivered to me by email. My top sponsors were happy with the results from my 2014 Tour, and they have asked me to do it all over again for 2015.

From this moment on, my mind will be caught up in thinking of ways to do things bigger and better, so that I may exceed my sponsors' expectations. I try not to look out too far into the distance, but instead to concentrate on one year at a time.

I am not saying that this plan works for everyone, but I have found that it has provided me with the passion to look forward to every year and to live in the moment as much as possible. It also has left me with no long-term goals, other than the social norms of acquiring a beautiful home, wife, kids, etc. For now, these take a backseat to traveling, riding, and discovering new things.

After suffering 3rd degree burns during a failed Guinness World Record attempt, I never thought I would be headed out for a 1st and 2nd national Tour.

My first Tour was a goal I set out for in order to give my mind and body something to aspire to and train for in recovering from my accident. My second Tour is the result of putting in a lot of work and being successful with the first Tour. I believe the key to a great Tour is to make sure that I put a lot of energy into every show and go the extra mile even when you are too tired. I want to make every Tour better than the previous. At the same time, I try to remember that each year could be my last, so above all, try to have fun.

For my 2015 Tour I acquired a 32-foot RV, three stunt bikes and a physical trainer. I practiced new stunts, and built a new custom stunt bike. Every stop on the tour is planned to be a party. When the RV shows up, the entertainment shows up.

I want spectators to be blown away by the stunts, the RV, the motorcycles, the promotional girl, and the spectacle of it all.

I like to capture amazing videos and photos for my social media and travel to some of the biggest and most beautiful cities in the U.S. I like to leave my sponsors speechless at the results of each tour.

It was not even halfway into 2015 and I was already busier than I have ever been in planning the summer tour. In April 2015, I received a call that was highly unexpected. It was a production company, asking if I would be willing to try to regain my Guinness World Record on TV this year. Here I am, looking forward to an already busy year, and on top of it I am being asked to risk my life again on national television!

I was almost in shock that they would ask me. My father told me years ago that the way extreme sports are headed is that, in order to capture people's attention on a mass scale, one must be willing to risk life and limb for simple entertainment. This couldn't be truer, as I nearly died in my second attempt at a World Record and now I was being asked to do it all over again.

The production company explained that I have a great back-story and history with this World Record and that they believed it would pull in ratings.

I am not normally one to back down from a challenge, but while I was recovering in the hospital after my failed attempt, my father gave me a piece of very good advice.

He told me that I don't have fear like most people do, so I need to go forward in life with a bit more caution. I need to check myself because I am willing to risk more than most people, and I had just seen how this could mean the end of my life very quickly.

With this in mind, I found it easy to say no to the production company—not only because I don't think it's doable on two wheels but also because it's not important for me to break this record. I don't care about the attention, I don't care about the money, and I especially don't care to try and appease everyone. I enjoy my life the way it is, without having to risk it on national TV.

The production company even went as far as to offer me a higher payout, but I replied with a simple yet easy way to understand my outlook on the situation:

"It's hard to spend the money if I am dead."

Besides, I have more pressing issues than to try and burn to death.

I'm in the middle of building my custom stunt bike to take on tour. I like to travel with multiple bikes, so that if I have issues with one, I can grab another and continue performing.

In 2014, I built the ultimate stunt bike by building an Aprilia stunt bike, which was the first of its kind. For 2015, my plan was a bit different, as I decided to build another custom stunt bike—but this time by tearing the whole bike apart to start from scratch. I wanted to incorporate something new that nobody has ever seen, so I decided to have a custom tube frame made and to have it chromed. I also decided on using a purple and chrome theme with this bike to really grab people's attention. A few people along the way, including the chrome plating company, told me it was not the best idea to chrome the new frame and that it was cheaper to paint or powder coat.

The build had taken me a few months but now I was nearly at the end, and it was coming together nicely. I was hoping it would look and come out the way I had planned it in my head.

As I multi-tasked with a bike build, tour, events, and my new RV, I was feeling like a circus clown, juggling everything at once but at the same time remembering to have fun with it.

I am honored to be able to ride for a living, and in return I do my best to keep it that way. Do I think I will be riding forever?

No, I plan on exiting the same way that I entered this sport…fast and strong.

There are other things for me to discover out there in the world, especially outside of the motorcycle industry. I would like to be known for other things than riding, and even if I am not, I will always have my memories to remind myself that I took a chance in life and reaped the benefits from it.

I wasn't afraid to take a leap of faith by choosing a dangerous career and leaving a cushy job. I know that deciding not to get married and settle down was ultimately the best choice for me at that time in my life.

This story isn't about a little kid with a dream of becoming a professional freestyle sportbike rider. My life has been about doing my best and being happy while doing it.

The memories I have from my past 10 years of riding mean more to me than any job title, new car, or amount of money.

Since I was young, I have been lucky to have the support of my family. My father taught me how to work on bikes, took me riding as a kid, and was really there for me, as a father should. I had love and support, but just as importantly I had a mother and father who could be strict when I pushed the boundaries.

My father taught me to be the best man I know how to be, and he did that without even needing to tell me so. Instead, he has shown me, through the person he is and the way others speak so highly of him. I wish that someday I can be half the man that he is. My mother and I have always had an up and down relationship. She has always expected a lot of me, through my early childhood and even still to this day. I would say that my mother has pushed me to succeed in life and to never take no for an answer on something worth fighting for. I learned from her unwillingness to give up on things and applied it to my life, whether it's in school, riding, or obstacles in life, and for that I am truly grateful to have her in my life.

My brother Ben continues to support my riding and my choices in life. He has been there for advice and has been a great person to look up to. Having an older brother who has lived such a clean lifestyle meant that I never strayed too far from my moral compass as a kid or as an adult. He has looked out for me in fights and in life. He is one of my biggest fans, and in return I am his.

2015 Tour was one for the books, with 20 events in 60 days and covering 7,000 miles. There was a specific day during the tour that I will never forget. My friend Kendra was putting together an event in Alabama for Big #1 Motorsports, but what started out as a simple bike night ended up as me performing for a group of kids from the Make-A-Wish Foundation in Birmingham.

Kendra asked if I would be willing to lend my services to perform for 12-year-old Colby Buchanan, diagnosed with Cystic Fibrosis. As the event got closer and I physically got closer to Alabama, I learned that more kids from Make-A-Wish were signing up to come out, and by the time I got into town over 30 kids had signed up, along with their families. The news and newspapers had gotten wind of the event and so had my sponsors. Speed & Strength sent out a helmet to give to Colby, as well as posters, stickers, and Dunlop hats to hand out to the rest of the kids. On the day of the event, I was on the local news along with Colby to promote the event and to bring awareness to the local Birmingham Make-A-Wish Foundation.

When meeting Colby for the first time, I noticed how strong a kid he was. There was no feel-sorry attitude coming from him. He was fully aware of his condition, but he didn't let it stand in his way. After the interview I presented him with his helmet and shirt and told him I would see him later at the event.

Later that evening, bikers started arriving along with the families of the 30 children. I had never done anything like this before, and I wanted to try my best to at least put a smile on everyone's face for one night. It was not as though I could do anything to cure them physically, but I was going to do everything I could to bring a positive light to the evening. Earlier that day my promotional model, Kayla, put together 50 gift bags filled with stickers, posters, and hats for the kids.

Before my first performance, Kayla and a few volunteers at the event handed out the bags to each of the families. As I began getting my riding apparel on for the first show, I looked over to the kids and felt something come over me. This wasn't a group of kids screaming, fighting, and yelling at each other. They were calm, collected, and patiently waiting.

I had the opportunity to do something special this night, and I was ready for it. I introduced myself to everyone over the PA system and fired up my bike.

As the motor started, I could see some excitement in the kid's eyes. I started the show with a few wheelies and simple tricks. I wanted to keep the pace nice and slow for the first show. After I completed my first show, the kids made their way over to my rig for autographed posters. I took pictures, signed hats, and answered questions until it was time for my second and last performance for the evening. This last show was going to be different. I wanted to take up the energy this time around and to bring Colby out to the middle so that he could be a part of the show.   This time around I was doing wheelies up close to the fence, doing huge burnouts, and then I nodded to Kayla to bring Colby into the middle of the performance area. I began to drift around Colby, and he didn't have a drop of fear in his eyes. Why would he?

This kid battles Cystic Fibrosis like a champ; he wasn't about to be scared of me!

I will never forget the moment I was drifting around him, and when I looked up to see his reaction, he looked into my eyes and had the biggest smile on his face. I'm not one to be emotional, especially while riding, but this struck a chord with me. It was a joyful and authentic smile that seemed to match exactly the way I was feeling. It was as though time slowed down just for that moment. I drifted off to the corner of the lot and finished with a huge burnout to light up the dark sky with smoke.

The line at my booth was long. Everyone at the event was doing their best to help out with the food, music, and festivities. I was happy to sit there as long as it took for every kid to get a poster and pictures.

There was one specific young girl that came up to me with excitement. She wanted to let me know that she enjoyed the show very much and that her favorite part was the burnouts. What was unique about this little girl was the fact that she had recently become blind from a tumor in her head. She wasn't complaining about not being able to see the performance. She was in fact happy to tell me about how much she enjoyed the experience of listening to the scream of the engine and the smell from the burnouts.

She was explaining the show through her other senses with excitement in her face. This was the second moment of the night that hit me hard.

These kids were dealt a bad hand but were making the most of it and doing their best.

I wish more of us would do the same with our lives. After the events I usually pack up the rig and head out for the next show, but this one was different. I was still taking in the evening's experience and had decided to camp out that night at the shop. I stayed up late that evening talking with Kendra and Kayla. We had dinner in the rig and looked over the photos and video from the show.

As I pounded down my dinner, I remember looking at the two of them and feeling a sense of pride. I was proud to be a part of something special that night.

Six months later...

My two-month tour was a success and I completed 2015 with 35 events nationwide. Could I be doing so well that I could reach my final goal? Could I obtain my dream of becoming a factory rider?

Perhaps this meeting I have with Kawasaki will go well.

Clint Ewing is a professional sportbike freestyle rider based in Southern California. He graduated from Sonoma State University with a degree in Business Marketing and is currently performing nationwide. Plus he has a really cool dog named Apollo! You can find Clint at www.clintewing.com

Recovery after second World Record attempt

Make-A-Wish Alabama

Laguna Seca performance

Limo Bus in Guam

Just before my run in with the real police

Young Ewing riding at Castaic Lake

Stall Jump

NHRA Performance

Night out in New Orleans with Kellie

Niagara Falls

One for the record books

Best part of riding

34234826R00061

Made in the USA
San Bernardino, CA
23 May 2016